Jim the Swim

Jim the Swim

A Story of Determination to Live Life to the Full

James Anderson O.B.E.

authorHOUSE

AuthorHouse™ UK
1663 Liberty Drive
Bloomington, IN 47403 USA
www.authorhouse.co.uk
Phone: 0800.197.4150

© 2015 James Anderson O.B.E. All rights reserved.

No part of this book may be reproduced, stored in a retrieval system, or transmitted by any means without the written permission of the author.

Published by AuthorHouse 11/17/2015

ISBN: 978-1-5049-9405-7 (sc)
ISBN: 978-1-5049-9406-4 (hc)
ISBN: 978-1-5049-9407-1 (e)

Print information available on the last page.

Any people depicted in stock imagery provided by Thinkstock are models, and such images are being used for illustrative purposes only.
Certain stock imagery © Thinkstock.

This book is printed on acid-free paper.

Because of the dynamic nature of the Internet, any web addresses or links contained in this book may have changed since publication and may no longer be valid. The views expressed in this work are solely those of the author and do not necessarily reflect the views of the publisher, and the publisher hereby disclaims any responsibility for them.

This book is dedicated to my parents,
whose love and encouragement from the very start
has allowed me to have such a full life;
and to my brother, Stuart,
who included me in all his exploits while we were growing up,
my disability making no difference to him.

Contents

Preface ix
Foreword xi

Early Days 1
School and Work Centre 9
Holidays and Hobbies 19
Training and Preparation 30
Barcelona 1992 40
Atlanta 1996 51
Sydney 2000 61
Athens 2004 73
Beijing 2008 85
London 2012 98
Random Thoughts 113
Acknowledgements 117
A Day with My Dad in the Mercury 119
The Auld Year's Nicht 123

About the Author 129

Preface

When I gave up competitive swimming, I had a desire to write down my story. Due to my cerebral palsy, I have problems with reading and writing, as well as unclear speech. So writing a book would be problematic. I was sitting in church one day when I spotted a lady who I knew did drama, and I thought, *Maybe she would help me*. I approached her and asked if she would be willing to help, to be my hands to get my tale down on paper. She told me she would think about it and then came back later in the week to say yes. That lady is Sally North, a retired occupational therapist.

When we first started, I was a bit wary of her because I had had mixed experiences with occupational therapists over the years. I wasn't sure how I would get on with this one. We quickly gelled, however, and I soon found out that she had the same sense of humour as my parents and me. I dictated the book to Sally, a process she describes as my words going into her ear, down her arm, and out of the end of her pen. The words are all mine; she has not interfered at all with the content of this book. I have shared with her good times and bad in my story. Sally has been angry on my behalf at times about some of the situations I faced. We have had sad days and days when we had to stop because we were laughing so much. Because of the concentration required by both of us, we managed about two hours per session before fatigue set in, and Sally typed up the results in between sessions. It has been a great learning experience for both of us.

But on to my tale. …

These are the only words in this book, apart from the foreword, that are not Jim's. Because of Jim's lack of oxygen at birth, the part of his brain that makes the connection between reading and writing did not develop properly. By way of compensation, he developed a great ability to remember where we were in the book and was able to tell me where on each page he wished to add to or alter the text. As I read back the page, he was able to calculate roughly how far down we were by how many words I had used. His mental organisational skills are amazing, and as someone who has to make lists for everything, I have found working with Jim both inspiring and a great pleasure.

Sally M. North

Foreword

I first met Jim Anderson at a Commonwealth Games dinner in Glasgow in 2004, after the Athens Olympics and Paralympics. The dinner was part celebration of successes and part fundraiser. I was thrilled to have returned to Scotland with my first Olympic gold medal, won in the 1-kilometre track time trial. Winners had been asked to take their medals to show to guests at the function. I discovered that Jim had not one gold medal but four from the Paralympics, including two won in world-record times in his chosen sport of swimming. Later that year, as the previous year's holder, I was able to present Jim with BBC Scotland's Sports Personality of the Year award.

It has always been a pleasure to meet up again with Jim at various sports-related events over the years, including parades of athletes after major championships, and Jim was present at the ceremony when I was given the Freedom of the City of Edinburgh. I know only too well how much effort is needed to attain international selection, gold medals, and world records: the slog of training, putting a social life on hold, and the discipline. Disability sport is no different from able-bodied sport in that respect, and Jim has excelled at British, European, World, and Paralympic Championships for many years.

Well done, Jim, from one retired athlete to another.
Thanks for sharing your story.

Sir Chris Hoy

Early Days

Apparently I made a dramatic entrance into the world on Easter Sunday 1963, a second son for John and Brenda Anderson. I arrived six weeks early, feet first, and by way of an emergency caesarean section, as I was suffering from lack of oxygen. Because of the emergency, a consultant was called in. She had been pruning roses in her garden at home and arrived in a flowery frock, over which she put a plastic apron. After I was born, the consultant said that Mum was lucky to have two sons, but later when it was clear I was very poorly, she said Mum was lucky to have two because she may end up with only one. Craigtoun Maternity Hospital in St Andrews was my birthplace. Dad always said I was born in a field. Even yet, I never close doors behind me.

Soon after my birth I was taken in an incubator to the Victoria Hospital, Kirkcaldy, and Mum was kept in hospital in St Andrews to recover from her operation. The first time my mum held me was when I got home four weeks later. I cannot imagine having a baby and having to wait four weeks before even picking him up. Nowadays that would never happen. Mother and baby would be in the same hospital and at least be able to see one another, and the father would be able to see both on one visit. In our situation, my dad was racing between hospitals on his Lambretta scooter. My brother, Stuart, and Dad stayed with our gran, who we called Ferm Gran, at Easter Kincaple Farm while we were in hospital. Dad was working all day with Granddad, who was a gaffer at Easter Kincaple.

Mum was used to handling Stuart, a strapping toddler close to two years old, but I was only five pounds, three ounces when I got home. I was long and skinny, like a skinned rabbit. They told Mum and Dad I was mentally handicapped and would not be able to cope with anything. I had some difficulty swallowing and sucking, so getting milk into me was not easy. It took two hours hard labour for my mum to get me to finish my bottle, and that with a two-year-old running round. Mum got me on to solids quickly by making pink blancmange, which went down easily. One day when our doctor, Dr Delaney, called, Mum was feeding me the blancmange, and he called it "Windolene pudd". Mum fed me my Polio serum by mixing it into the pudd. Not that I remember any of this of course.

Yes, I had difficulties as a child, but my parents treated me the same as my older brother since there are less than two years between us. I was included in all that was going on in the family. I was baptised on Stuart's second birthday in Holy Trinity Church in St Andrews, although I don't remember that either. Mum said she had a christening cake for me and a birthday cake for Stuart to save any arguments. Mum's sister Auntie June was my godmother. In fact, when we were very young Stuart and I were like the Queen. Just as her Majesty has her date birthday in April but an "official" birthday in June when weather is thought to be better for official celebrations so we brothers had different birthdays. Ferm Gran would always give us both presents on the other's, so it was like having an official birthday in addition to our own.

We moved from Easter Kincaple to Kirkton Barns for about six weeks, and then Dad got a new job as a gaffer at Coal Farm in St Monans. One year the family went to the Fife Agricultural Show, and the owner of Coal Farm bought a brand-new tractor. Dad was very excited that he got to drive it all the way home.

One of my earliest memories is of being in the living room in the cottage at Coal Farm. Mum was making a Christmas cake and brought a table into the room so she could keep an eye on what we boys were up to. Stuart was sitting on a stool at the table, and I was sitting in my high chair by a big coal fire. I can still see that coal fire in my mind's eye. We were fascinated with the sights and smells of the cake. On one of Stuart's birthdays Mum made a cake shaped like an army tank, using chocolate finger biscuits for the gun. I can still taste the chocolate icing. I remember playing in the garden with Stuart and being propped up with pillows because my balance wasn't very good at that stage.

Later on when I was able to, I sat on the bunker in the kitchen, watching Mum making dinner. We had dinner at dinner time and tea at teatime in those days. Dad started work at 7 a.m. and came in for dinner at noon, so Mum would be in the kitchen by 11 a.m. You see, she had a wee radio about the size of a cigarette packet, and every day we would listen to *Waggoner's Walk* at 11 a.m. and then *Jimmy Young*. In the afternoons we would watch *Watch with Mother*. My favourite program was *Andy Pandy*. After dinner Mum would tidy up and get the dishes washed. On good days we would go out for a walk, me in my pram and Stuart walking or on his scooter. Along the country roads it was quiet, without much traffic. Mum would spot bits of wood or fallen branches and would load up my pram to take the wood home for the fire. I didn't get much of a view. What a way to treat a "poor wee disabled boy", loading him up with firewood!

Sometimes Dad had to help milk the cows and would start at 3 a.m., and some weekends he had to take a turn at feeding the animals. Stuart and I would go with him when he brought the cows in for evening milking. There was an occasion when someone on the farm was ill and Mum went to help with the tattie dressing. I remember kneeling on tattie sacks, watching the tatties going into the hopper. At that time, part of Dad's wages was a pitcher of milk (about four pints) every day, fresh from the cow. None of us is any the worse for it. Nowadays everyone is so conscious of heat treatment and fat content.

We had mobile shops too in those days. The Co-op Bakery had a horse and cart, and Uncle Geordie came from St Monans once a week with his fruit and veg lorry. Mum was learning to drive as well, and Dad made her practise reversing up and down the farm road for hours at a time, with me in the back.

We had two grannies and two granddads: Dad's parents we called "Ferm" Gran and Granddad because they lived on a farm just outside St Andrews, and Mum's parents were "Toon" Gran and Granddad because they lived in St Andrews. Ferm Gran came to see us on Tuesdays, and sometimes her sister Auntie Maggie, who lived in Elie, would meet her at Coal Farm, about midway for both of them. I remember sitting on the bunker, hanging over the wringer, waiting for Ferm Gran's bus to arrive. Ferm Gran always had sweeties in her message bag. Even when we boys got older, we would still rummage in Gran's bag to see what she had brought for us. Sometimes my mum would say, "Ferm Gran's not coming today". She would have some farm job, like dressing tatties, to do.

We went into St Andrews on Saturdays about three o'clock to see Toon Gran, Toon Grandad, and Auntie June. We would have a cup of tea and then go up the street shopping with Toon Gran. She came back with my favourite thing, a cookie round. We often went into a grocer's, and I can still smell the coffee beans. Toon Gran always shopped in old-fashioned shops because she hated supermarkets. When she paid for her milk in the dairy, there were lots of churns of different sizes and a lovely fresh, clean smell. Sometimes Stuart and Granddad would go to a football match. In winter Auntie June, who lived with Toon Gran, would wrap a tartan travelling rug round me to keep me warm in my chair. Stuart and I would go into Woolworths and Mum and Dad would buy us sweets. We boys were spoiled rotten. There was a real toyshop in St Andrews too. Auntie Ise lived in a flat over the toyshop, and that was where Dad was born. Years later we were in St Andrews with my brother and his daughter Judith, and my Dad said to his granddaughter that the mark in the road, which really marked the site of a martyrdom, actually marked his birthplace! We loved that toyshop. I would buy farm animals, and Stuart bought kiltie soldiers.

Toon Granddad had his own special chair by the fire, and I was allowed to sit behind him. There was a bookcase beside his chair which always had a bag of chocolate eclairs on it. When we were on holiday during the week and I was with Granddad, we used to listen for a man coming down the road shouting, "Telly! Telly!" He was delivering the Dundee Evening Telegraph. On Saturdays Granddad had to go and get the sports version, the Saturday Pink, to get that afternoon's football results.

All our Fife family came to us at Christmas, but at New Year's Toon Gran would have the whole family, including Auntie Betty and her family from Balfron, to New Year's dinner. She had a large round table that could extend by putting extra leaves in. It was Stuart's job to open it up with a spanner. Thirteen of us sat down round that table, and Toon Gran would serve a big pot of chicken soup, home-made steak pie, and a Christmas dumpling. I have never tasted chicken soup like my gran's.

In the summer we met up as a big family again, and had huge picnics at Craigtoun Park. We had a baker in St Monans who made the best snowballs. They were huge and creamy. One picnic when Auntie June was eating one, Dad and Uncle Jimmy pushed it in her face and then picked her up by her arms and legs and swung her round. Auntie June yelled for them to stop. She enjoyed fun, but she was always a bit of an "old maid" and liked to keep her dignity. There was also a miniature railway in the park, and Mum would take me on her knee for the journey. What fun we had!

One year at Christmas, Stuart and I were given a game called Hands Down. It involved putting your hand down quickly, like Snap. Mum, Ferm Gran and Granddad, Stuart, and I played. Ferm Granddad was never quick enough to put his hand down, and we were all helpless with laughter. I remember sitting in my pushchair when we went to see Mum's friend Mrs Howie. We called on a Monday before we picked up Stuart from the school. I used to play with Mrs Howie's daughter, who had dolls. We had great fun, and one Christmas I cried because I hadn't been given a doll. I cried so much that I was given two, which I called Leslie and Peter.

We had other celebrations during the year as well. At Halloween we would dress up in the house and dook for apples. Mum always made sure our heads were pushed into the water so we ended up all wet. On Bonfire Night we'd have fireworks and a bonfire in the field opposite. Mum, Stuart, and I made a Guy using my old clothes.

On Sundays we would go and see Ferm Gran. She went to bingo on Saturdays, and we boys would go to her holding out our jumpers in the hopes of sharing in any winnings. In the afternoon we would play cards, the game we called "Horsey" (better known as Newmarket!). Stuart and I both learned to count while sitting on Ferm Gran's knee playing Horsey. Those Sunday mornings she would bake a bannock and treacle scones for us. Ferm Gran did a lot of knitting too. She used to hand Stuart and me her knitting patterns and ask us to pick one she could knit for us. Then she would bring out an enormous bag of wool, and we could pick what colour we wanted. I used to like green for Celtic. At that stage I was quite young and didn't know anything about football, but I always chose green. There was a picture of the Royal Family as well, and a young Prince Andrew was wearing a jumper with a Fair Isle yoke. Gran knitted us both Fair Isle jumpers after that.

On hot summer's days we would go out for a walk through the cornfields, with poppies growing in, over to Monksholm where Ferm Gran got duck eggs. We'd pick cobs of corn from the field edges too. Stuart and I saved up coloured foil wrappers from sweeties and Easter eggs, and Mum would wrap each grain on the ears of corn in the foil to keep for Christmas. Ferm Gran had a huge garden with strawberries, raspberries, and blackcurrants. She would give us baskets of fruit to bring home with us for jam-making. When Mum didn't have enough sugar in the cupboard, it was a quick chase to the shop the next day. In the summertime Ferm Gran would make my favourite meal of mince, new potatoes, and fresh garden peas. Then she would bring us a soup plate full of strawberries. Sugar would arrive in a bag, placed in the middle of the table, and we'd top it all off with a tin of Carnation Milk. At that stage I didn't like tomatoes, but Ferm Gran dipped them in sugar and I soon learned to eat them.

Sometimes we went to see Great-granny at Kettlebridge. I remember sitting on Mum's knee in the back (no seat belts in those days). Dad was driving and Ferm Granddad was in the front, with

Ferm Gran, Stuart, Mum, and me in the back. I remember Great-granny as a wee woman. She had a fascinating cuckoo clock. We "men" would go along the road to get ice cream and sweeties while the women made the tea, usually a fry-up because Great-granny loved it. Uncle Chay, who lived with her, was never able to make it right. Great-granny's house had a lean-to at the back with the kitchen, a toilet, and a bath in it. It smelt horrible, and the smell turned out to be creosote. Uncle Chay had built the lean-to himself from old railway sleepers. There was a piece of red and white gingham round the sink to hide what was underneath.

Mum used to shop in St Monans and often went into Helen Butters's wool shop. Mum would sit me on the counter. I would fidget, and Helen told me I would fall through into a big bag underneath if I didn't sit still.

When I was about four, we had a family holiday at Butlins, Ayr, and Mum had knitted three jumpers for Dad, Stuart, and me, all the same with reindeers round the bottom. There are family photos of us all on the hobby horses in our "team kit". I loved the roundabouts and other rides, but Stuart wasn't so keen. We are close but different. Soon after we got back from Butlins, Stuart had to go into hospital for two weeks. I don't know how Mum managed. In the morning she took me from St Monans to my grans', Ferm Gran and Toon Gran day about. She spent the afternoons with Stuart at Cameron Hospital in Windygates. Then she came back to collect me to prepare meals for us for that night and the next day. She also bought a comic every day for Stuart, rolled it up, and posted it to the hospital so he could have something to do in the mornings. Summers seemed to be warmer then. Two of my cousins used to come for the summer holidays, and we spent lots of time on Elie Beach. After dinner Mum would quickly do the dishes, and then we would go to the beach for the afternoon. Mum would still have to support me in the sand while we played. It is strange, in retrospect, that the local fishermen said I should be put in the sea water, as it would strengthen my legs.

Watching me grow up, Mum and Dad didn't really believe I was mentally handicapped, and I, aged about two, demonstrated this when we were on our way home from a holiday in Fort William. We went past Ferm Gran's house, and I howled because I recognised the place and we hadn't stopped. We spent that holiday in a caravan, and it rained solidly for a week. That was when I learned to sit up by myself. After we got home Toon Granddad bought me a wee supportive chair, which I still have. I learned how to get up on my knees when I had measles. It seems that every time I was unwell I learned a new skill. When I was getting near school age, someone from Fife Council came to do a preschool assessment to see where I should go. They referred me to the Royal Hospital for Sick Children, Edinburgh, known to locals as Sick Kids and at the age of four I was diagnosed as spastic (now known as cerebral palsy).

School and Work Centre

When I was five, legally I had to be in school, and with my mobility problems the best solution was thought to be the local nursery school in Cellardyke. Mum used to drive me, and my chair, there every morning. I was a bit frightened because I felt safe at home in my wee cocoon. Nurseries in those days were intended for children whose mothers were working and who required day care. I was the oldest child there. My brother and cousins had all gone straight to the village school. The main thing I remember of the nursery is the beds, with little blue and pink blankets, where we were put down for a rest in the afternoon. But I didn't think of myself as a baby!

I started getting physiotherapy and speech therapy at home, organised by Rillbank at Edinburgh Sick Kids' hospital. This unit specialised in cerebral palsy. For two years I had six-monthly assessments by a paediatrician, an orthopaedic surgeon, and a psychologist. I apparently once amused the psychologist in a word association test. He said "straw" and I replied "cows", being a country boy. The usual answer was something like "drink" or "glass". His tests showed I had above-average intelligence. Every six months my parents told me I would get a milkshake on the way home from Rillbank if I was a good boy. I generally did!

These tests in turn allowed me to get a place at Westerlea School, Edinburgh, which the Scottish Council for the Care of Spastics ran. The school only had forty-eight openings in total for the whole of Scotland, and I was awarded one of them. Before I started at

Westerlea, I got a letter from the headmistress, Miss Mathams. She wrote it on bright-red paper because, she said, it was a happy letter to welcome me to the school. Westerlea had a residential unit, as it took pupils from all over Scotland. Mum and Dad made the decision to move from Fife, where Dad was a gaffer, to Turnhouse Farm, on the outskirts of the capital, where he became a tractor man. That change allowed me to stay at home and travel daily to school from age six. Mum and Dad must have loved me so much to move home and job, leaving my grans and granddads in Fife. We used to walk along to what is now Edinburgh Airport every day to get our paper, the *Dundee Courier*, and our comics. One day our neighbours gave us a shout to go down to the farm road's end, as the Queen was coming past. That was the first time I saw the Queen and Prince Philip. I never dreamt I would one day go into Buckingham Palace. As a schoolboy that thought wasn't even a dream. Going to a new school was not easy. A driver used to come and get me but I cried every day for two years on that journey. Eventually Mum took me, but it didn't get any easier. I was a right girny bairn when I went to school. My teacher during the holidays before my second term sent me a letter. It said that if I managed a day without crying or even just girning, I would get a gold star, and if I managed a whole week, she would take me down to the cafe for an ice cream. I managed a whole week and got my ice cream, but the next day I started to cry again and never managed a second ice cream.

I hated school. I remember being strapped into my desk. It felt horrible, but I suppose some pupils needed more support than others. All the students had different difficulties and individual timetables for our therapies, which included physiotherapy, occupational therapy, and speech therapy. I got to know everyone else's timetables and used to keep the teachers right. The occupational therapists (OTs) did dressing practise with us, but I used to help some of the other students and was never ready myself. Being in a specialist school with individual programmes allowed us all to develop as much as possible.

I do not agree with the practise of integrating all disabled children into mainstream schools. They cannot always get the special support services they may need to grow physically, socially, and emotionally. Scottish schools in the 1970s automatically provided services like those offered by Hungary's Peto Institute in the 1980s. A "special school" can offer better stimulation, support, and challenges. I believe that disabled pupils in mainstream classes are not always pushed to achieve their potential.

As part of fun at Westerlea we put on a concert every year, and I was always excited when that time of year came round. Every class did something different. Miss Mathams's class always did a toyshop window song, and we got to be toy soldiers, teddy bears, and dolls. One year I was cast as someone going on an outing to the shop to buy something.

I love Scottish history, which all started when I was eight years old. Miss Mathams did a term on Mary, Queen of Scots, and Mum took me and three classmates up to Edinburgh Castle. We saw Queen Margaret's Chapel and the great hall, and I was hooked. Other excitements were the annual fete of the Scottish Council for the Care of Spastics (later renamed Capability Scotland). A large marquee was erected at the bottom of the gardens, much to the entertainment of the pupils, and teas were served in Murrayfield Day Centre. At Christmas we were encouraged to make gifts for our families. We made waste-paper bins out of catering-size cans. I made a footstool for Toon Gran out of two biscuit tins covered in fabric, with pieces of carpet on top and bottom. Toon Gran liked a nap in the afternoon and had broken her ankle, so it proved very useful. One year I made a cushion. I turned the handle of the sewing machine while the classroom assistant guided the material. Mum received a jar decorated with shells.

I was in Miss Mathams's class for four years. She took the youngest students and taught us the basic three *R*s, as much as we could manage. We were in classes of twelve, with one teacher and one classroom assistant. The classroom assistants moved round each term. We used a peg-board system for doing sums. The assistants would get our worksheets from Miss Mathams in the morning and would help us work through them. In the afternoons they would prepare work for the following day. They used to pin the worksheets onto boards using drawing pins, and to this day I have a phobia of drawing pins.

After Miss Mathams's class, I moved on to Miss Dick's class for the next two years. Miss Dick had had polio and was affected down one side. In the summer if the weather was warm and sunny, we took our desks and went outside wearing big sunhats to do our lessons. Every year at school we had our eyes tested, and I hated it. They put drops in our eyes, and I couldn't see a thing for the rest of the day.

Miss Dick thought that, as I had difficulty in reading, I would believe that everyone in the class would be better than me. That is why I went into Miss Plenderlieth's class when it came to secondary school. Miss Plenderlieth's class was aimed at the less able stream. We did less academic work, and I found it frustrating because I wanted to learn more than crafts and going on outings, no matter how educational. Nowadays easier methods of communication and teaching have made this situation less likely. Despite being in this stream, when I was twelve I wrote a story about going out with my dad for the day in the delivery lorry. Unknown to me, my teacher had sent it away to a national competition organised by the Spastics Society. I was sitting in the classroom one day having my milk and biscuits. Miss Plenderlieth was off ill and wasn't there when Miss Mathams came in to class with my mother, who worked in the school kitchen. I wondered if I was in trouble, but Miss Mathams said she had a letter and asked Mum to open it. Mum asked what it was about. She read it and discovered that I had won the competition, the first Scot ever to do so, and the Spastics Society was inviting me to go to London to receive my prize. What a pleasant surprise. Poor Mum didn't even know about my story. The letter read, "Judging has now taken place in the Literary Contest, and I am very pleased indeed to advise you that your entry, 'A Day with My Dad in the Mercury', has won first place in the schoolboy section of the contest." The judges for different age groups were Gordon Honeycombe, an ITN newsreader; Keith Waterhouse of the *Daily Mirror*; and Merry Archard, a children's writer who judged my section. Her assessment of my piece said, "James took a lot of trouble; he has the ability to detach himself from his own troubles and his own situation ... a born writer."

I was sent for by Archie Cameron, chief executive of the Scottish Council for the Care of Spastics, to be congratulated on my achievement. His office was at least two floors up, and there was no lift. Mum had to carry me all the way up, just for him to shake my hand and say "Well done." What an effort for my mum, when he was more able to come down to us. He was put on a pedestal by everyone and could do no wrong, but he was just a man!

Mum, Dad, Stuart, and I went on our very first visit to London to collect my prize for my story. We stayed in Fitzroy Square at the spastics council's assessment centre. It was 1977, Jubilee Year, and the city was all decorated. We went on a city bus tour with Miss Mathams. We visited Westminster Abbey and the Tower of London. The queues to see the Crown Jewels in the tower were enormous, but a beefeater opened up a gate and let us in to see them. He put a stool inside the rope beside the glass case and told me all about the gems. Needless to say, he was a Scot.

Our friend Ina Greenock from Broxburn had got a congratulations card for me and knew that Mary Wilson, wife of the then prime minister, was doing the presentation. Ina posted the card to 10 Downing Street and asked Mrs Wilson to pass on the card, which she did. My Mum was black affronted! Mary Wilson had just become a granny to twin boys, and Miss Mathams thought it would be good if the school could make a small gift to the boys; two little soft toys and white heather posies. It was the wrong time of year for white heather, but Mum was able to get some from a specialist grower. Miss Mathams said the Anderson family would never let her down. One night Miss Mathams invited us to her hotel for dinner. When we got there it seemed to be a big posh hotel. Nowadays I would think nothing of it, but then it was very special, a wee boy in a wheelchair in this huge dining room. Miss Mathams was so excited, she showed us all round the place, acting like the lady of the manor.

It was Broxburn Gala Day soon after we came home from London, and the Boys' Brigade (BBs) always put in a decorated float.

Having seen London decorated for jubilee, Mum thought it would be good to do a Rule Britannia theme, and Ina Greenock was Britannia!

Usually if you won the writing competition one year, you were not allowed to enter the following year. However, I had moved up an age group in that year, and the next year I came second with a story called "Milkman" about a bairn being born handicapped. People read it and had tears in their eyes. We went to London again and met Mrs Wilson once more. Jean Rook was the judge this time. I went on to win another first for my story "Auld Year's Nicht", judged by Mrs Denis Healy, and a second for a story I called "Family Gathering", judged by Nina Bawden. I wrote my stories using Scots words, and Miss Plenderlieth had an awful problem understanding some of them. We bought her a dictionary. "Milkman" and "Auld Year's Nicht" were both published in an anthology of stories, and I was also published in *Scottish Home and Country*, the magazine of the Scottish Women's Rural Institute. It all helped with the pocket money!

I got a good all-round education at Westerlea. Miss Plenderlieth even went on an outing to the farm where Ferm Granddad worked, for a project we were working on. I remember our teachers as "old dearies", all single ladies living with their mothers. Miss Plenderlieth's Christmas card was always signed from her and her cat. She wore her hair up in a bun. In my last year at school, the mould was broken. Miss Mathams had retired, and Miss Plenderlieth was promoted. My new teacher was Mrs Anderson (no relation!). Mrs Anderson was a younger woman with a twelve-year-old son at that stage. I learned a lot from her and wish I had had her earlier. I believe she educated us more than she simply occupied our time.

Miss Dick used to organise a weekly charity coffee morning at school, and we took in money so we could buy baking or plants potted up in yoghurt pots. Mum was not too delighted when I came home every week with a smelly geranium. One of the classroom assistants, who was in the Salvation Army, would teach us the wrong words to songs when Miss Plenderlieth was out of the room. She felt we should have the experience of doing something naughty, something normal for wee boys. We loved the Christmas carol "Not Well, Not Well!" for instance, and as for Shepherds washing their socks, well …

I used to dislike going to speech therapy because the therapist would put a small wooden spatula in my mouth to hold my tongue down and ask me to make sounds. The physiotherapists (physios) made me walk in bare feet. I didn't like that much either because the floor was always cold and never a carpet in sight. Joy Blakeney, one of the OTs, came back from a cerebral palsy conference in London excited about seeing the children swimming. She started a programme of swimming for us, using the pool at Donaldson's School for the Deaf. I was about nine and remember being involved in that first small group. The OTs used the activity for dressing practise, and the physios liked the exercise benefits. The edge of the pool was quite rough, and they made us crawl to the water. I always came home with skinned knees, but it was all in the name of independence. At that age I just thought it was cruel. I can now see that if they had assisted us all, we would never have been as able as we are today. One day a week after school, Mum took me to the pool at Graysmill School. There were two students who gave disabled children one-on-one attention in the water, making it good fun.

Once a year we had to attend a clinic with Mr Fulford, an orthopaedic surgeon, but he never really got to know me, as I never needed surgery. I still had to go because the physios wanted me to have a rollator, a walking aid on wheels. The first one I had fixed round my waist. I used to be a wee devil with it. There was a long corridor at school that we went down for our meals. I would build up speed on my rollator and then lift my feet and freewheel as far as I could. The housemothers used to shout at me all the time.

My favourite pudding at school was chocolate blancmange with brown sugar on top. I'd have two platefuls, and Mrs Smith or Mrs Mackie would feed me and make sure I ate every last drop. My pet hate was being made to take soup through a plastic straw, not always pureed and sometimes with lumps of vegetable.

On one occasion Prince Philip, Duke of Edinburgh, came round the school for a prize-giving day, and I was at OT when he came in.

I had to take my clothes off and get into a paddling pool just to show what I could do for myself. He must have wondered what on earth we were all up to. There were three of us in the paddling pool, and boys being boys, we threatened him with our water pistols. Prince Philip put up his hands in surrender. A *Daily Record* photographer captured the moment and won an award for his picture. Nowadays we would need parental permission, disclosures, children's permission, and all sorts for that to happen. I don't know how they cope in special schools now with all the rules and regulations. When Miss Mathams had story time, there was always one pupil or another cuddling in while she read. We felt safe at school and loved by most of the staff.

At primary school I won my first swimming medal, for managing a breadth of the pool at the school for the deaf. The medal was made out of cardboard and ribbon and was very special. I remember sitting with Ferm Gran one hot summer's day watching David Wilkie winning gold with a world record in the 200-metre breaststroke at the Montreal Olympics, thinking to myself that I would love to do that one day. It was all a lovely dream. I had never heard of the Paralympics at that time.

Another achievement came when I managed to swing on a swing in the school grounds all by myself. I also became interested in wheelchair dancing. At first I was team mascot because I was too wee and couldn't manipulate my wheelchair well enough to dance. I love music to this day and was very disappointed that I couldn't take part properly. When I did get into the team, we were entering competitions. My first competition was in London. This was not only my first competition but also my first time away from home without my family. I cried for the whole weekend. I cried myself to sleep. Finally, then, my housemother got some peace when I dropped off. We stayed at Baden-Powell House and danced in the Hammersmith Palais. With the school team we also danced in Glasgow; at the Albert Halls in Stirling; and at Usher Hall, Queens Hall, and Assembly Rooms in Edinburgh. Both my grans and my aunt came to Stirling to support us.

I left school at sixteen and went on to New Trinity Work Centre. My interest in wheelchair dancing continued when I moved to New Trinity, and our team danced in the Scottish championships in the Beach Ballroom, Aberdeen. We did demonstrations as well as competitions, and once we had an international competition in Glasgow celebrating twenty-five years of Scottish Disability Sport. I did some solo disco-dancing there as well as team dances. I was actually Scottish wheelchair disco champion for eight years, and every year I had to have a new outfit. Mum would watch *Come Dancing* and Torvill and Dean for inspiration. She spent hours sewing on sequins and glittery thread. She would usually start with a gaudy shirt and decorate from there. The man playing Pharaoh in "Joseph" at our church borrowed my white outfit. In November of 1993 I went down to Cheltenham overnight by bus with an Edinburgh team of wheelchair dancers. I won the British Disco Dancing Championships wearing a very glittery outfit! When we went to that competition in Cheltenham, we actually stayed in the hotel that was used for the set of *Crossroads Motel*.

For the International Year of Disabled Persons our team was invited to perform at Cornton Vale, the Scottish Women's Prison. It was all very strange going into jail. As part of the women's prerelease programme, they organised a concert, and our group became part of it.

At New Trinity I did a lot of gym work and tried out different sports. Sometimes we went to Meadowbank for activities. I did wheelchair dash, wheelchair slalom, and throwing the club; all good for general fitness. I even represented Scotland in wheelchair slalom at a competition in Newcastle. Six of us travelled down and back in one day in a minibus from the centre. At that time cerebral palsy sport was encouraged and big in Scotland. There were a lot of centres like New Trinity all taking part in national events, whether it was athletics, swimming, boccia, wheelchair dancing, or other activities.

I was taking part in local swimming galas and doing work on static bikes and weight training at New Trinity, but there were problems ahead. I had been very active and jumpy in my movements, and always on the go. Mum described me as "a hen on a hot girdle". However, at the age of twenty-six I developed severe back pain. I couldn't walk. I couldn't sit up. I just curled up into a wee ball, frightened to move because of the pain. Nobody believed how bad the pain was, and some people thought it was all in my head. I was prescribed pain killers, but they barely touched it. Eventually after taking X-rays, doctors discovered I had developed arthritis in my spine and hips. It took months but it did gradually settle. After six months of hell I was referred for physiotherapy to learn to walk again and to be able to get back upstairs to my bed. I had slept downstairs during this time. The physio also took me into hydrotherapy to improve my muscle power with less stress.

There was one benefit from my time of illness. To keep me occupied, Mum got me to rattle down old jumpers to make stuffing for cushions we still have. It not only kept me busy but also greatly improved my dexterity, and even now I can pick up the smallest object. Those months of inactivity changed my metabolism, and I had become less mobile. When I was able to get back to New Trinity, they were all very kind. Jim Thomson encouraged me back to swimming, but I was reclassified from CP6, being fairly mobile, to CP2 because of my loss of mobility and fitness. That change helped, and I haven't looked back since, as my story will show.

Swimming was not the only opportunity we had at New Trinity. One day my friend Edwin and I went with Jim Thomson to Dunfermline College to try a sport new to us. It was boccia, a bit like the French game of boules but played with softer balls. People with all levels of ability can play it, and it is now a Paralympic sport. In 1993 I entered the British Boccia Championships in Easterhouse, near Glasgow. Somehow my competitive spirit came to the fore, and before long I found myself the national champion.

I attended New Trinity for twenty-six years, leaving there in 2004.

Holidays and Hobbies

We moved from Turnhouse when I was about eight. My brother and I had bunk beds, me in the bottom one. I was always scared that Stuart would fall on top of me, and I didn't like looking at the underside of his mattress. Mum and Dad found a large picture of a red Massey-Ferguson tractor and stuck it under Stuart's bunk. That helped! I loved sitting with Dad on the tractor or combine. I had a tricycle in those days, and we used to go along the road to feed donkeys in a nearby field. Mum had to attach reins to my trike so that she could pull me along if I ran out of steam.

We used to have lots of family holidays and went twice to Rothesay. As a wee boy I felt we were going abroad because we had to go on a boat. We sailed from Wemyss Bay, and as we drove down the Clyde, Mum would always sing "Sailing Doon the Watter fur the Fair". At the weekends the road was mobbed with people travelling back to Glasgow, as we always went on holiday at the end of the Glasgow fortnight. As the ferry approached Rothesay all you could hear was the Alexander Brothers booming out from the loud speakers on the pier. We stayed in a caravan on a farm, and the farmer always wore a "Frank Spencer" beret. I remember spending hours roly-polying down a grassy slope with Stuart and crawling back up to start again. At a Sunday school picnic in Edinburgh, I spent the afternoon roly-polying, as it was something I could do by myself, without help, while the others ran races. At night in Rothesay we went to the local arcade and played prize bingo and the penny machines.

The car we had at the time was a leaky Mini. All Minis seemed to have rusty floors in those days, and our one had cardboard and bits of carpet over the holes. Stuart and I sat in the back with our feet up to stay dry. One of the cafes in the town wouldn't allow us in because they didn't let "prams" in. Even though Mum explained that mine was a wheelchair, they wouldn't change their minds. We enjoyed spending our money somewhere else! As a family, we enjoyed the local ice cream in a top-hat cone (a chocolate snowball on top).

Dad was reading a Sunday paper one day and saw an advert for a tent, and he bought it. It came all kitted out with sleeping bags and cooking equipment. The day it arrived was very wet, but we were so excited, we pitched it in the living room. Our first trip in it was up north to Glencoe. I cried for a whole week because I didn't like the feeling of being closed in by the hills and the bleakness. I was all right when we got to Beauly where it was flatter. After Beauly we moved on to Aberdeen. It seemed everywhere we went Dad bumped into school cooks he knew from his delivery of fruit and vegetables to their kitchens. We met one in Aberdeen who had brought her ferrets with her. Mum refused to stay on that site in case they escaped during the night. Sometimes we went to Burntisland when the shows were on. I was allowed to play prize bingo, the kind where you slide a cover over the numbers rather than use a pen. It was very useful for my finger coordination.

We went down south, down the west, and up the east. When we were in Dorset the beach nearly got washed out from under us by the tidal current. Mum had to keep pulling me up the beach away from it. In the morning I woke up in our tent and Stuart was nowhere to be seen. There was a slight slope in the campsite, and during the night he and his sleeping bag had slid down almost out of the tent.

On our way back north, still camping, we went to Scarborough and walked along the seafront. Going past a theatre, Mum got very excited because there, up in lights, was Val Doonican's name. We went to see his summer show and managed to get front-row seats. Mum spent the evening in a swoon. On another trip we went to Blackpool, and I was in stitches all night at Tom O'Connor's summer show, a real family show. It was all good clean fun. In Blackpool we also saw *Joseph and the Amazing Technicolour Dreamcoat*. Jess Conrad played Joseph, and his coat filled the whole stage. It really was amazing. When we did *Joseph* in Broxburn Parish Church in 1992, Mum used some of the memories of that Blackpool show to help with costumes. That church show was the first time I was aware of being part of the church family. We all just mucked in together.

One summer the house we were renting was being modernised. Mum and Dad were getting fed up living in perpetual mess. On the spur of the moment they booked a holiday in Jersey. That was the first time any of us had been in a plane. In those days you travelled in your Sunday best. When we arrived at our guest house, our landlady told us not to unpack because it was the Festival of Flowers on the seafront. She said we should go down and see it. The parade was really beautiful. I got a great view because I was so wee at the time that I sat on my dad's shoulders. It was very hot on our first visit, and Stuart, Mum, and Dad slept on top of their bedcovers. Apparently I slept under the covers, hugging a hot water bottle. Stuart got his back badly sunburnt, and Mum and Dad got the tops of their feet burnt. Having travelled out in Sunday best, they came back in flip-flops because it was all they could wear.

On a second visit to Jersey we hired a car. Dad often went the wrong way, and we always seemed to end up in an area called St Peter's. On one Saturday we went to a summer fete in the grounds of a manor house. We parked in a field that had loads of daffodil bulbs in it. Mum managed to "acquire" quite a few of the bulbs and put them in her bag. We had to smuggle them home because you are not supposed to take bulbs, plants, or cuttings off the island. The evidence can still be seen around Broxburn. At that fete I had my photo taken with Miss Jersey, the singer Stuart Gillies, and the Chipmunks. Stuart was sixteen and accidentally fell over a concrete bollard in the street, skinning both his knees. He had to spend his holiday in shorts with sticking plaster on both knees, definitely not cool for a teenager.

After the tent we bought a touring caravan and travelled all over Britain. I do remember though that we often went to St Andrews. Instead of going south, Mum would say, "Where are we going?" and we would head for Craigtoun Park. At that time my great-aunts were still alive, and they would come over for afternoon tea parties. All the summers seemed to be warm then, and I sat in our awning listening to my music tapes. We did venture farther away too. I remember a very hot trip to Lincoln. I was in the back of the car with the windows open. I had a wee tape recorder and listened to music all the way. My favourites at the time were Barbara Dickson singing "Caravan" and Cliff Richard singing "Miss You Nights" The very first song I recorded was "Seasons in the Sun" from Ed Stewart's Saturday morning radio programme. We had a boat trip on the Humber too, and there was a mass of ladybirds covering everything. It was quite a sight. We went to Canterbury, but Dad again took a wrong turn somewhere and we ended up going through the middle of London, towing a caravan. The cathedral in Canterbury was being restored, and Mum rescued a piece of the stonework, which she still has, from a skip. While we were there we went on a day trip to France. There was no problem with access to the ferry, although two crewmen came to get me up on deck. They took the wheelchair and left Dad to carry me up a narrow, steep stair. Going over was flat-calm, but coming home we had to walk round and round on deck. It was so rough that if we stopped moving, we all felt seasick.

We went to Stamford Bridge Caravan Park, which was a site that I could get around on my rollator. It was the first time I had seen a weir on a river. I loved just watching the water rolling over it.

Mum and Dad were BB officers at the West Church in Broxburn, and I was a member of the junior boys section for ages eight to twelve. I managed to get my gold award by completing educational, physical, and spiritual tasks. I even did some basic gymnastics with a little help, and the other boys fought to have a shot in my wheelchair while I was trying to do forward rolls. I had to learn the Apostles' Creed and even lay a table. At a parents' night some of us dressed up to sing the Calum Kennedy song "Five Lovely Lasses from Banyan" in tartan skirts and with ribbons in our hair. We went to a BBs weekend camp in the church hall at Balfron, where my auntie Betty stays. Mum did the catering for camp, and on the Friday on our way home from school, we used to pick up bread and pies at Anderson's, the bakers, in Broxburn to take with us. All during the week beforehand, our house was full of camp food. It was about the time of my birthday in April, and Auntie Betty always used to make a clootie dumplin', with pennies in, for all the boys. It was a big dumplin'! The BBs had a football team too, and Mum helped with transport to games. Nat Beggs, who took the team, asked me to become team mascot because I was watching anyway.

I was also in the Westerlea Scouts. I remember we went to camp near Glasgow and it was snowy. The bus got stuck, and the scout leaders had to take turns to carry me on their backs for several miles to the camp. I went abroad for the first time when I was fifteen, to a scout camp in Norway. We had great fun fundraising for the trip, holding coffee mornings, jumble sales, and raffles. We also had a sponsored walk, and I managed to raise £18.20p. Mind you, I was pushed for 10 miles round the Meadows in Edinburgh by a student from Telford College. We flew to Denmark through a storm over the North Sea and had six hours before our onward flight to Norway. We went to the Tivoli Gardens, where I went on the big wheel, at that time one of the biggest in the world. The view out over Copenhagen was fantastic. Tivoli looked like it had been invaded by scouts as a Glasgow group was on its way home from a Danish camp. On our way back to the airport, we passed the Little Mermaid. In Norway we were camping under canvas, but it rained and it rained and it rained and we were in a sea of mud! The Scout Leaders had to dig drainage ditches round our tents. The cooks' tent was flooded, and they had great fun making our packed lunches, up to their ankles in running water. At breakfast we had the most wonderful strawberry jam with our bread. It was so thick and full of fruit but came in packets like milk cartons, instead of the jars we were more used to.

Because of the conditions, we were moved into a local church hall so crowded that I imagined it was like the Blitz. The scouters on duty had to go back to sleep in wet tents because there wasn't enough room for everybody in the dry. They spent their time in swimming trunks. We just stayed wet! I was in mud and rain, and meanwhile my parents and brother were enjoying a hot summer in Jersey! On our way back we spent some time in Oslo and were taken up a very tall tower to look out over the city. The views were spectacular, but we spent more time there than was intended because the lift broke down. We took greetings from the lord provost of Edinburgh to the lord mayor of Oslo and shared haggis and oatcakes at a final reception.

A year later I got my Queen's Scout award. One of the things I had to do was a 6-mile night hike at Aberfeldy. I did it with a friend who was also doing a badge. He sat in my wheelchair while I pushed it for the 6 miles. Unknown to us at the time, our scout leaders were observing us and keeping in touch by walkie-talkie to make sure we were safe. I was awarded my Queen's Scout at camp in Aberfeldy.

It was a complicated week because I had to come home on the Friday. My cousin was getting married. Mum and Dad picked me up, towing a touring caravan because they had been on holiday in Kenmore. They stayed in the caravan in the camping field on the Thursday night. Ferm Granddad was also taken into hospital in Dundee at the same time. We came home and went to the wedding, where my cousin Betty married Ian. Then on Saturday we had to go back to Aberfeldy. Mum and Dad dropped me at camp, went back to St Andrews to pick up Ferm Gran, and visited Ferm Granddad in hospital; and then all three came back to Aberfeldy to see Colin McKay, district commissioner, present me with my Queen's Scout badge. My Ferm Granddad died in August that year. It was like the end of an era for the family.

Before I was fifteen I had been going to Sunday school. I knew about Easter, but it never registered; however, when I was fifteen I went to a Good Friday service. Elaine Gilmour sang a song that really touched me. It was "I Don't Know How to Love Him" from *Jesus Christ Superstar*. I felt so emotional about Jesus dying, and that was when I really became a believer in God and His power. All the stories fell into place. About that time, STV was showing the series *Jesus of Nazareth*, and I became emotional about how they could crucify Jesus. I decided at the age of about twenty-two that I wanted to join the church. I had grown up going to Sunday school and Boys' Brigade, but the time was right for me to take that next step of full membership. Apparently there wasn't a dry eye in the congregation when I did, but thankfully I wasn't aware of it at the time.

Mum and I used to go to the Royal Highland Show, taking a picnic with us. Our first call was always the flower show. For the rest of the day this "poor wee disabled boy" had his wheelchair laden with Mum's purchases. I loved going into the farming museum. I loved looking into the old rooms because I saw things that Ferm Gran had in her house and things I'd been told about. It reminded me of her living room and her putting her washing in the oven to air. The museum gave me my inspiration for a play I wrote when I was about sixteen. It was called *Bothy Nichts*. Traditionally, unmarried men working on farms were accommodated in bothies and had to provide their own entertainment. They used to invite girls working in local houses for parties and sing-songs. The tradition of bothy ballads and poetry developed, and my play was based on such a gathering. It was put on at the church, and we had to put it on twice because people liked it so much. We had to build an extension onto the stage in the church hall. My Dad danced a sword dance wearing nicky tams. We were all a little worried that he might go through the extension. The play was also put on at an end-of-term concert at my old school, a year after I left. Mum and I were invited back to see it. At that time too, the woman's guild put on a Christmas party for both men and women pensioners at the church. Mum and I wrote pantomimes and sketches and sorted out songs for community singing. I wrote a sketch called "The Knitting Bee", performed by the Scottish Women's Rural Institute and the church, and once at the end of a silent auction to let a wider group of people see it. I wrote a comedy sketch roughly on the theme of "Keeping Up Appearances". Among the performers was Mrs Moyes, our minister's wife. Rehearsals took two hours instead of one because Mrs Moyes and my mother are gigglers. The older people always liked to have a good laugh each year. One year we did Cinderella with a *Grease* theme, and Mum and Ina Greenock's party piece was "Nobody Loves a Fairy When She's Forty".

The United Nations declared 1981 International Year of Disabled People. West Lothian sent some people on a ten-day holiday to Germany as part of their celebrations. I attended the local PHAB (physically handicapped and able-bodied) club in the early eighties. It was like a youth club for people with all different kinds of disabilities, and I was one of the group sent to Germany. The day before we travelled, Mum, Dad, and I went into Edinburgh for the festival cavalcade. It was about the time of Prince Charles's marriage to Diana, and the Girls' Brigade had made a float with a wedding theme for Broxburn Gala Day. Someone from the cavalcade organisers had seen the float and asked for it to take part in Edinburgh.

On the Germany trip David McWilliams accompanied me as my carer. I had met him through the PHAB club. Every day for ten days, we went on trips; one was to see one of the dams the Dambusters attacked. The whole trip seemed like it was coffee, cakes, and apple pie all the way. The nearby church bells woke us every morning at five o'clock, and we were totally exhausted by the time we got home.

There were lots of activities at the PHAB club, including Halloween parties and coffee evenings, and once a year we went to a camp. I went to one Halloween party dressed up as Hilda Ogden. Ferm Gran leant me a crossover pinny. I had rollers in my hair and a headscarf. One year we went to Butlins, and that is where I got my teenage drinking out of my system. I have never felt so ill in all my life. We had camps at Dalguise, Haggerston Castle, and near the Lake of Menteith. David couldn't go to them all because he was working. One year the camp happened on my birthday and some camp staff tied me to a farm trailer and left me for a while; a dastardly act by a health visitor and a bank manager! I came home on a Tuesday afternoon, tired and excited, ready to tell Mum all about it, but my mother was in the kitchen. She was up to high doh because the next day was the annual competition of West Lothian "Rural" federation. All her entries were coming out of the oven "not good enough". She had to make more and more and more till she was satisfied. Instead of asking me about my exciting camp, she was anxious about her baking.

As a group we went on a sponsored walk, fundraising for *The Edinburgh Evening News*'s children's charity. I was quite thin then, which is just as well because David had to push me up Arthur's Seat. David and I also went to collect a cheque at the local bowling club when, while coming home at one o'clock in the morning, we were stopped on the main street in Broxburn by the police. The police officer asked me if I knew who it was that was pushing my wheelchair. It turned out they were worried I might have been kidnapped from a local hospital. That happened after a hospitable Friday night, and on the Saturday I was involved in a sponsored swim. Never, ever swim with a hangover!

We also used to go camping with PHAB Scotland at the Trefoil Centre just outside Edinburgh. It was somewhere that people couldn't sleep because of my snoring, a problem of which I was unaware at that time. We still made lifelong friends through PHAB. I also started to attend the Splash Club in Broxburn, a swimming club run by parents for people with disabilities. We had outings, and one of my favourites was on the Seagull Trust's canal boat, based in Ratho. Latterly we went on a week's holiday to Pontin's in Blackpool. My mum and dad took a ride on a rickshaw bike. They pedalled round and round as I sat in my wheelchair taking my ease. What a laugh! One outing we went to Butlins at Ayr, and Mum and her friend Fiona went on the hobby-horses; what an embarrassment! But the Splash Club helped me a lot with my swimming career.

I was invited to my first garden party at the Palace of Holyroodhouse because I had been to Germany for International Year for Disabled People. Mum and I were all dolled up, but the car wouldn't start. We phoned Dad at work and asked to borrow his work one. We got it but were running a bit late. We put on Radio Forth to get local traffic reports. Bill Torrance, another good Broxburn lad, said everyone would be parked by now because nobody went late to garden parties. "That's what you think," said Mum. We got there and actually parked easily, getting into the grounds just as the Royal

Family was coming out. Because I was in my wheelchair, people stood aside, and we found ourselves at the front beside some Girls' Brigade officers. Prince Charles had come along the row and was about to turn and go back when one of the Girls' Brigade people said, "One more, Your Royal Highness". He came to speak to Mum and me as an extra. Our Broxburn friends asked us to bring back a wee doggy bag of goodies from the tea. We managed sandwiches, but not cream cakes, as they had to go in Mum's handbag!

Thinking of handbags, we had a jumble sale at the church, and there were a lot of handbags. I was manning the stall with a box for the money. An old dearie put a coin in my box and said, "There you are, son. There's a penny for you," and walked away without taking a bag. I never did get that penny, because the organisers took it all in at the end.

Dad used to have a week or two's holiday in January, and we would enjoy going away to get a bit of winter sunshine. For four years running we went to Tenerife. I used to love the thought of all the people at home shivering in snow while we were walking in the sun. One of my best memories is going out for a meal to a restaurant bar and having a lovely meal while listening to a man singing "Guantanamera", all very Spanish. One year we went to Ibiza. On our way back, Mum was going frantic. She and Stuart were on the plane, but Dad and I were still in the terminal. They had been bussed out to the plane, but Dad and I weren't allowed on the bus and had to walk on the tarmac all the way. Another year when we came home, Dad had to get back to work the next morning delivering potatoes to Ayr: one day in sunshine and the next up to his knees in snow.

As I grew up I hated looking like a disabled person. We all seemed to have the same haircut and wear the same clothes and were expected to behave in the same way. So I rebelled a wee bit. At the age of nineteen I wanted to get my ear pierced. I was fed up and wanted something different. I didn't really think I'd be allowed to, but Mum marched me down to Broxburn, the town where I live, and the deed was done! A hairdresser who comes to our house permed my hair as well. Now that was a change of image.

In 1998 Stuart married Helen in Plockton in the north-west of Scotland. The family all travelled up in two minibuses. Dad drove one, and my cousin Ian drove the other. I was best man and wrote my speech, although I handed it over to a friend of Stuart's to deliver. It was another great family occasion. It was very windy because of the unfortunately named, given the circumstances, Hurricane Helen. Mum's friend Fiona's hat took off in the wind when she got out of the minibus, but worst of all, when Helen was leaving her parents' house the wind blew the door shut, trapping her veil. Her father didn't have his house key and had to go to a neighbour for a spare, leaving Helen stuck there. She was soon released though, and the wedding could continue. Our family weddings seem to attract incidents. At my cousin Margaret's wedding in Balfron, Mum tripped going in, her hat went flying, and she had to find somewhere to wash the grass stain off her knees.

Training and Preparation

Before I take you off on my travels and the excitement of competitions around the World, I want to tell you a little about the hard work necessary to get there. It isn't just a case of turning up and getting in the water.

As a child I had learnt to swim using a rubber ring, with Mum and Dad at the Commonwealth Pool in Edinburgh. They had taken my brother and me for fun and a splash-about. I had started swimming a little more seriously at school, still using an inflatable ring, and enjoyed it. We had annual school galas that included races for people who used assistive devices such as armbands and rubber rings. These races happened in Lothian-wide galas for schools and centres, and in cerebral palsy games at national and even at international levels, some people still swam with the assistance of armbands. In some ways I wish this still happened, to encourage those with more severe disabilities to take part, both for enjoyment and for healthy exercise.

When I moved on to New Trinity after leaving school, I was asked what I liked to do. I mentioned swimming, and it became part of my activity programme. It was really New Trinity that encouraged my swimming. They organised sessions at Warrender Baths, David Wilkie's home pool, for anyone who wanted to go. It was a 25-metre public pool. Jim Thomson from Trinity, a remedial gymnast and head of CP Scotland Sports, became involved at that time. I was still wearing the ring to swim. Jim gradually let the air out of it until it was flat. He eventually said, "B****r this. I'm getting rid of the ring." I had been too scared to go without it, but Jim made me and I never looked back. As time went on we changed to swimming at Jewel and Esk Valley College's pool, another short-course pool. I also joined the Splash Club in Broxburn and began to show some ability. We wrote a letter to the local paper asking if there was anybody who could take my training forward and got a reply from an elderly lady who helped with some coaching. Tam and May Naples at the Splash Club took me in hand and got me swimming competitively rather than just having fun. They got me swimming in local galas, and it seemed that every time I got in the water my times improved. From these local galas I was invited to join the Lothian Swim Team. I went to annual galas in Glenrothes, my most serious gala at the time, and took part in these competitions for ten years.

I was swimming and training quite happily until my arthritic condition took over and I had to be out of the water for about two years. Following physio and hydrotherapy, I did manage to get back to the Splash Club and back into the Lothian team. The Lothian team competed in national competitions, and at one of these competitions in Ayr I was invited to become a member of the Scottish squad – all very heady stuff! I was so excited and honoured. This happened in April 1991, and in May I went to my first Scottish training day at Lochgelly. I got the biggest shock of my life. Before this I had swum for about half an hour, doing about 500 metres, but that day I swam for two hours. I couldn't move for two days afterwards.

For competition I had been classified as CP6, but after my illness I was reclassified as CP2. All competitors in disability sport are given a classification according to their abilities so that people can compete against others of a similar standard. I had to step up my training programme because international competitions are generally in 50-metre pools. I only swam twice a week, doing about 500 metres per session in 25-metre pools, but on a Sunday the 50-metre Royal Commonwealth Pool in Edinburgh was given over to swimming clubs for training. One lane was dedicated for disability swimming. I couldn't get over how long it took me to swim 50 metres without a break. I could only manage about ten lengths in an hour. In the 500-metre training swims there was a little work on leg kicks and the rest was arms. If we felt tired, we just gave up! Pete Wyman was my coach, and all he told us was to get in the water and swim the distance. I didn't have a training schedule to follow at that time, just a lot of ploughing up and down pools three times a week. I did do a little "land" work on a static bike that was expected to strengthen my leg muscles and improve my stamina. It all felt very serious at the time and was sufficient to win medals. Cliff Carrie became my coach, and he set up a training programme, which Dad worked through with me. I was invited to go to train with Richard Brickley for two hours once a month at Glenrothes, instead of Lochgelly. That's where I met Paul Noble, Kenny Cairns, and others who have since been friends for years. We trained hard and built up friendships at the same time.

Prior to 1984 each category of disability held its own sports (e.g. amputees, spinal injuries, the blind, and so on). In 1989 the organising committee for the Barcelona Paralympics decided to try to develop a "universal" classification of disability system for use at their event. The committee made an attempt to bring together all disabled athletes of similar disability, whatever the cause, so they could compete together. Each competitor would be assessed for his or her ability and be allocated a level. In 1990 there was a trial swimming event in Holland to refine the system. Inevitably there were teething problems and disputes over classification, but these have generally been resolved as time has gone on. The classifications were in use at the European Championships in 1991 and at the 1992 Paralympics, both in Barcelona. In those days the classifications were numbered from 1 to 12, with 1 being the least able. My classification was 2. As a swimmer, that became S2, defined as swimmers with severe coordination impairment in the trunk, legs, and hands, and mild impairment affecting the arms. These swimmers move through the water using mostly their forearms and shoulders.

At Glenrothes I trained in the same lane as my friend Alan McGregor, one of my closest rivals at the time. He was also classified as S2, but our rivalry was only in the water. I qualified at Darlington for the European Championships in Barcelona, the year before the

Olympics. At those championships we S2s were not expected to warm up before races or warm down afterwards. They thought the extra metres would tire us too much. We were "poor disabled people" who shouldn't be pushed to achieve, and yet we still broke world records on minimal training. All that was expected was that we should be put in the water, swim as fast as we could, and be fished out at the end. After Barcelona and for some time afterwards, we still went to Glenrothes once a month. Drill work was added to my training to add to the range of movement in my shoulders and strength in my arms. It made getting up Monday mornings to go to New Trinity very difficult. I was always tired, sore, and stiff.

In 1992 Cliff Carrie from Trinity, who coached all sports, became my coach for five years; but when Lottery money became available and coaching became more demanding, Cliff believed he couldn't give me the necessary time. To justify getting funding for training and competitions, you had to submit your training schedule every week. This was to prove you were "earning" your money. I had to buy a computer and sent my dad on a course to learn how to use it to send paperwork to British Swimming. Mum became my personal secretary and dealt with all my entry forms, booking hotels for competitions in Britain, making travel arrangements, and organising carers for when I was away. Mum also dealt with non-swimming invitations to events, meetings, ceremonies, and presentations that came in once I was an international swimmer. I had to pay my carers a wage as well as travel, accommodation, and food expenses while we were away. Although they were called carers, they became more like pals, and once the work was done we were free to do whatever we wanted: sightseeing, reading, chatting, or just chilling in cafes. My carers did, however, have to be part of the core staff of the British team and be available for other duties if necessary. It was no holiday for them.

In early 1997 I had a minor setback before going to a competition in France. I developed anaemia, lost weight, and was very tired. I was put on iron tablets and did no work for six weeks. I then had to rebuild my stamina and fitness bit by bit. Jim Thomson organised a new swimming coach for me, Don McFarlane, who was with me from 1997 to 2003. Don was a coach for able-bodied swimmers. Jim Thomson had set up a disabled club in Loanhead, Midlothian, and suggested that I go along one night a week. Instead of coaching me from the side, Don coached me from the water. One night he was stood behind me and shouted "go", and I missed his eye by an inch. He wrote a training programme for me to follow at Trinity and the Splash Club. When I first met Don, he asked me what I wanted him to do. I said I wanted to become a world-record holder. Through hard work and determination, it happened. In one race in Christchurch, New Zealand, I swam my fastest ever 50 metre and fastest ever 100 metre before setting the first ever 200-metre world record for disabled swimmers. I later went on to repeat the feat at the Athens Paralympics. At around the same time, Paul McInneny came on board as my carer.

Training camps in Darlington for the British squad were added, under head coach Patsy Coleman. She stood at one end of the pool and shouted that everyone was to do sixteen 800 metres repeats. I said I couldn't do that, because it would take all day. At that time I was doing about 1,000 metres in total per session. Patsy's response was "If it takes all day, it takes all day!" She was "easy" on me but still insisted I did six 800 metres. It was all hard work but paid off.

Before Sydney, lottery funding came in and technical support staff were employed. At our Australian Gold Coast camps, we were split into ability groups and I was given Eddie McCluskey and Jill Stidever as my coaches at the international level. Neither had dealings with an S2 swimmer before, so there was a lot of experimenting with kick boards and pull buoys to find out the best way to position me in the water and to find out what was right for me. They worked on my starts and turns, streamlining them and shaving seconds off my times. The other swimmers and I also did step-tests, which involve five repeats of 100 metres, starting fairly easily but gradually increasing speed until the last 100 metres was flat out. At the end of these our coaches tested our pulses and our blood oxygen levels to check our heart and lung functions. All the swimmers had to get out of the pool to have their ears pricked for a blood test, but not me. Spencer Moore, one of the testers, came to poolside to do mine. It was easier than pulling me out. For my entire swimming career I was always hauled out of the pool quickly to avoid delays in the competition. Regulations about manual handling nowadays makes that taboo, and perhaps that is why fewer people in lower classifications of ability are coming through to the elite level in sport.

Suddenly it was all very serious and like a proper job. Eddie used to tear his hair out with me because we trained in an outdoor pool in Australia. With no roof, I couldn't tell what direction I was swimming in and kept hitting lane ropes. Paul McInneny policed me up and down the pool, covered in sunscreen. We swimmers had to be lathered in sunscreen too before we went into the pool. At a camp in Majorca we wore small vests with monitors checking our fitness levels while we were swimming. The monitors fed back performance details to a central computer. The only problem for me was that I swim on my back. My chest got sunburnt in the outdoor pool, and by that night I looked like I was wearing a white bra.

Among the staff was Carl Payton, a bi-mechanical specialist. He used underwater cameras to analyse how people moved in the pool and where technical issues in streamlining and strokes could be improved or adapted. Carl and I are roughly the same age, and he still cannot get over me doing all this exercise at our age.

British Swimming had local squads for training purposes, and the Scots used to train in a 25-metre pool at Stirling University with Alan Lynn. However when we came back from competition in Sydney, we found British Disability Swimming had decided to start up four regional academies, in Manchester, Bath, Swansea, and Scotland. The Scottish one was to be opened at Stirling University with a new 50-metre pool. Lars Humer was appointed British Disability Swimming head coach, and the Scottish head coach was Kim Longden. To start with I only went to Stirling on Sundays, but in 2003 I cut down my days at Trinity. I went to Stirling Sundays, Mondays, and Fridays for training. I had been attending the Scottish Institute of Sport, Edinburgh, for physio on Tuesday evenings for some time prior to Stirling starting up.

In 2003 we started going to able-bodied galas, particularly in Sheffield and Manchester, where races for disabled swimmers were included. Finally in June 2004 I gave up New Trinity altogether and became a full-time athlete. For eight years I attended Stirling four days a week and one day at Broxburn Pool following Stirling's training regime. Broxburn Pool was very helpful with my training, putting up a lane rope in a public session, to enable me to put in the mileage without disturbing the recreational swimmers. I was swimming about 10,000 metres a week. At training camps, instead of five sessions a week, it was stepped up to ten with sleep in between. For those eight years at Stirling, my mother sat at a table, knitting, sewing, and doing crosswords, and Dad read the papers. My career kept the wool shop in business. Mum did a lot of cross-stitch wedding samplers and cards over those years and must have done thousands of crosswords.

My new coach, Anthony Stickland, stepped up my metres in training because I was concentrating on the 200 metre for Athens. I also started more bike work. Anthony helped me to win four gold medals at the Athens Paralympics. My coaches towards the end of my career were Rob Aubry and Paul Wilson, and my main coach was Kerry Wood. Each and every one helped me on my way. At one stage squad physio Paul Martin and squad doctor Derek Martin met with my Stirling physio. They suggested that I should sit on a big ball at home to improve my balance. The idea was that as I was sitting on the ball it would move when I did and I would constantly have to adjust my position to compensate. My biggest problem was that I had great difficulty getting onto the ball without kicking it out of the way in the first place. We managed by trapping the ball against my mother's chair, although this stabilised the ball more than was intended. I still have balance problems, but it did help at the time. I also had to lie prone for half an hour a day to help stretch out my back and hip muscles. I found it boring because I couldn't see anything going on around me. Fiona Gough, my Stirling physio, decided to strap me onto different exercise machines to improve muscle strength, particularly in my legs, and to help my coordination. Because of arthritis in my knee, I had to give up the static bike, but the physios got me a hand bike instead, which also improved my stamina and coordination. In 2004 all Anthony's swimmers went to the Moray House pool in Edinburgh to be filmed in the water. He wanted to analyse our movements underwater, which cannot be easily observed from poolside. The Scottish Institute of Sport paid for the project so that improvements in our techniques could be made.

After the Athens games I started doing warm-ups and warm-downs at competitions. It took a lot of time to work out how much time I needed to be ready but not too tired to race. Other swimmers hated being in the same warm-up lane as me because I have difficulty swimming in a straight line. In a race there is only one swimmer per lane, but in warm-up there can be ten all setting off at different times. Paul Mac and Paul Wilson used to walk up and down the pool shouting at me to move over.

When we are told a competition starts at 9.30 a.m., we swimmers have to be at the pool by about 7 a.m. to start our race preparation and warm-up. After warm-up, competitors have to enter a call-up area twenty minutes before their race. S2 competitors had to go into that area without a helper, so your escort, who would help you into the water, was not allowed to be in the room. If you needed help, you had to raise your hand and they could come in and help with things like hats and goggles, after which they had to leave again. The call-up area was where I listened to my music. Lots of competitors try to put others off, but that's where I went into my "zone" and often prayed for help in my races. Being in the call-up area was the worst bit of being an international swimmer, as pressure would build up. You would think after all the years it would get easier, but it got harder the longer I went on.

Warm-down, about ten minutes after a race ends, is meant to rid the muscles of lactic acid which builds up during physical activity and can cause stiffness and cramps. A warm-down usually starts fast and gradually slows down. Simple blood tests check lactic acid levels until the levels return to zero, or as close to zero as possible. Sometimes warm-down lasted longer than the warm-ups. At one competition in

Glasgow my race was one of the last, and I was still warming down as they were putting out the lights.

The whole science of sport medicine became involved in my training. I got more and more support from the Scottish Institute of Sport. They got me a land coach to improve my core strength, and weights work became more structured. Among other things, I did trunk-twisting movements with weights to help. Maybe I was trying to get big "guns" like Graham Edmunds! I also was allocated a nutritionist, Irene Riach. She wanted to weigh me but couldn't because I am not steady enough to stand still on a normal set of bathroom scales to register my weight. They purchased special scales that I could run onto in my wheelchair. They then deducted the weight of the chair, and that was it.

When athletes are in training they are regularly tested for any drug misuse, and Paralympians count in this programme too. These tests are done by a team of testers from the Anti-Doping Agency who can arrive unannounced at training sessions, at your home, and regularly at competitions. They once came to my house at 9 a.m. and left at 1.30 p.m. They have to stay with you until you provide the necessary urine sample, to ensure you don't tamper with it. It really is very difficult to perform with two strangers in the bathroom with you! The testers had been told almost my whole life history before they got away. They came to Broxburn Pool one Wednesday at the end of a training session. Mum was at a craft and chat evening across the road in the church hall, and to allow the pool to close up for the night I was escorted across to the hall to "wait" again. The testers that night enjoyed tea and biscuits while they waited. When athletes are on a world-class programme, they have to advise the agency of their training schedules and submit a list of their competitions every three months so that testers can find them at any time. You are given a little leeway to allow for emergencies, but if they cannot find you for testing after three attempts, you are not given the "benefit of the doubt" and can be banned from competing, as if you had "failed" a test. The lists were originally submitted in writing, but as technology advanced they demanded more and more information from competitors by computer. I found this very difficult, and if I needed to change any of my details, I had to phone my friend Graham in Wales to submit alterations for me. Luckily, we competed at the same events, so when he submitted his own he did mine too. It wasn't exactly convenient for either of us, but any changes, such as a weekend away, meant another phone call and a good blether.

I had dealings of a different kind with the Anti-Doping Agency. In 2006 I developed asthma, which was thought to be caused by prolonged exposure to chlorine in the water of swimming pools. I was tested for breathing capacity on a static bike in Sheffield, and Derek Martin, chief medical officer for British Paralympic swimming, prescribed inhalers for me. At that time any competitor on prescribed medication had to declare it to the agency and could be given a therapeutic use exemption (TUE) certificate. This would last for four years and would then be reviewed. Inhalers used by a healthy person can be seen as giving an unfair advantage, as they can open up the airways, allowing extra oxygen in. Asthmatics need inhalers at times just to get enough oxygen. When my TUE was due for renewal in 2010, an accurate reading of my peak flow was required. I have difficulty sealing my mouth round standard mouthpieces. Derek Martin and Paul Martin, the physio, who were up doing our annual medicals, brought different types of mouthpieces. Despite several attempts, my readings were not sufficient to satisfy the Anti-Doping Agency, who insisted I had to come off all medication. They did not believe I had asthma.

My times dropped off dramatically, and in training sessions I had to leave the water early because of breathlessness. I developed several chest infections and coughs without my inhalers, and at one competition in Manchester, Derek walked up and down poolside during my race to make sure I wasn't becoming too distressed. Eventually Brian Walker found a new piece of equipment, with which he was able to gain an actual reading from me. A very strong letter of evidence was sent to the agency, and after due consideration I was thankfully placed back on medication.

Barcelona 1992

I had the opportunity to go to Nottingham for a weekend of trying different sports. I tried athletics and boccia before getting involved again in swimming. My swimming improved greatly, and I went to a Scottish Disability Sport gala in Ayr, where I won a gold medal for my level of ability. It was my first national gala after my illness, and we were on the bus leaving for home when we were stopped in the car park by Richard Brickley, head of Scottish Disabled Swimming at that stage. He said he would like to take me to Darlington on the last weekend in June to a British-wide competition. I was so excited and couldn't wait to get home to tell Mum and Dad. It was a dream come true to represent Scotland. That was my first competition in a Scottish team, and I was given my first Scottish tracksuit. We travelled all the way by bus. My parents came down separately. The competition happened in the middle of our family holiday, so that was put on hold for a month. What a shock at my first British Gala when warm-up was at 7.30 a.m. It felt like the middle of the night. I got a fright too when I discovered that the pool in Darlington had timing pads on the lane ends. At home I turned using the gutter at the end of the pool. I would grab with both hands and push off again to go back up the lane. There was no gutter there, and I had to learn quickly, in competition, how to turn. I managed a qualifying time for the European Championships in Barcelona, a year before the Paralympics, in Darlington. When I got home after Darlington I started swimming widths at Jewel and Esk Valley to practise turning so that it would become second nature.

On the Saturday evenings at these galas there was a championship dinner and disco for everyone. Now I look back to that time and wonder how we managed to compete on the Sunday. We stayed at the King's Head Hotel, a place we were to stay for later training camps.

A few weeks later I got a letter inviting me to be part of the British team at the European Championships in September in Barcelona, but between the Darlington event and my selection for the Europeans, we had a bit of excitement in the family. My niece Pauline was born. All the excitement of swimming was topped off with the new arrival. In Barcelona I met a whole load of people I didn't know, and we were all put up in the Expo Hotel near the Central Station for ten days. All we seemed to eat was paella, for ten days! I can still see it, yellow in a bowl.

We were bussed to the pool, and the buses took us past Gaudi's unfinished Cathedral of the Holy Family. We really felt that Barcelona was a special place. They were still building the pool for the Olympics in 1992, and all you could smell in the warm-up pool was wet plaster. Before competition started I was given my international assessment. I was assessed in the water and on the physio bench and was given an S2 classification. This set what grade of race I would be in. I swam 50-metre backstroke and 50-metre freestyle, winning two silver medals. The 100-metre freestyle was a combined race, including S3 and S4 competitors as well. Unknown to me, the team manager, Carol Bradley, put in a successful protest to the organisers, saying medals should be awarded for each classification. After our meal that night we had a wee ceremony in the hotel. Peter Hull was awarded gold, and I won silver. I had won three silver medals at my first international competition, and I was over the moon. After ten days I was desperate to get home to show my parents my haul. Chris Holmes, a blind competitor, was also presented with his medal and was so excited he leapt up and managed to dislodge some ceiling tiles. Everyone was roaring with laughter. This meet was the first ever IPC (International Paralympic Committee) European Championships.

Back at New Trinity Pete Wyman coached me. He was into wheelchair racing, and now he had an international swimmer too.

It all happened so quickly: Ayr to Barcelona in the space of one summer. We had a British training weekend at Coventry, and in the foyer of the hotel there was an old black and yellow veteran car. The pool in Coventry at that time was also quite old. These training weekends were a shock. Instead of swimming once a day for thirty minutes, we had two two-hour sessions on Saturday and another two hours on Sunday morning. Jill Stidever coached me during the training weekend. I was so tired, but the coaches made me keep going and my stamina improved. We also had training weekends in Darlington, where we again stayed at the Kings Head Hotel. At the end of the weekend the staff took our bags to the station. The ambulant swimmers pushed the wheelchair users to the station, and these journeys developed into races. Unfortunately, Darlington Station is up a hill, so the last bit of the trip became very strenuous. I was all right. I was sitting down, but it was all very nerve-wracking.

In May of 1992 we went to Olympic trials in Sheffield, and I was to fly to Manchester from Dundee International Airport! I got the shock of my life when I saw the size of it. It was only a portacabin. And then I saw the size of the plane. Dad said I would have to pedal all the way to Sheffield, and Mum just roared with laughter. We flew down on a Wednesday afternoon and stayed in a hotel in the Peak District on our way to Sheffield. Our evening meal was a huge Yorkshire pudding filled with roast beef, vegetables, and gravy – difficult to eat but very tasty. The water in the pool at Sheffield was quite cold. In those days disabled swimmers were often given warmer water to swim in because it was thought that muscles would be looser in a warmer environment. However, this was an able-bodied meet, and it turned out that we were just a demonstration team. I felt we were just tokens and were on display.

There was a British short-course championship in Darlington in June where we were to try to get our qualifying times for the Barcelona Paralympics. In those days you didn't need to compete in a 50-metre pool to get qualifying times. There were not too many long-course pools around anyway. I don't know how some people managed to qualify on the Sunday, because there was yet another championship dinner on the Saturday night. How things have changed since those days. I got my qualifying times for my first Paralympics at that event, although I was so nervous until the letter confirming my selection arrived. Until that happened, I didn't quite believe it, and we were all so excited when it came through the letter box.

People gave the British Paralympic Association donations to help fund our team in Barcelona, and I was sent to Stirling University to pick up a cheque on behalf of the Paralympic Committee. I got all poshed up in suit and tie, expecting publicity photos and everything. When I got there it took all of two minutes. They just handed me the money and said bye.

When my selection became public the local church started to fundraise for a sports wheelchair for me to go to Barcelona. My NHS chair was very heavy and cumbersome. They had beetle drives, quizzes, coffee bars, and a sponsored swim done by Ian Scoular and me. BP Grangemouth matched the funds raised pound for pound.

At that time my family's favourite TV programme was "Keeping Up Appearances", and to thank Mrs Moyes for organising the fundraising, we invited Mr and Mrs Moyes and Matt and Jean Turnbull to the house for a "candlelit supper". They entered the spirit of the occasion by dressing up as Hyacinth and Richard Bouquet, and Daisy and Onslow. They giggled all the way up in the car, as they were worried they might be stopped. Matt was in his string vest, and Jean's hair was up in bobbles. Mr Moyes was resplendent in bow tie, and Mrs Moyes was wearing a huge picture hat – happy days before computer games!

In preparation for Barcelona the Paralympic team went to Stoke Mandeville to be kitted out. There, we slept in dormitory accommodation. The problem is that I am a snorer and no one in the swim team, apart from me, got any sleep. One night one person on the team wheeled me in my bed away to another room. I woke up the next morning wondering where I was. Now anyone travelling with me is supplied with ear plugs. My last carer would stay awake the first night so that after that he would be so tired he would sleep through anything. I remember sitting in the dormitory watching

Linford Christie winning his Olympic gold medal. The room was like a war zone, with kit everywhere. On the way back from Stoke Mandeville, we nearly missed the plane at Heathrow. Paul Noble ran through the terminal, pushing my wheelchair, and we just made it. I had to collect my suit from Next in Edinburgh, and while we were collecting it my parents' car was towed away because its front wheels were just out of the parking bay. We were standing in the street with me clutching my British Paralympic suit, and no car. We had to take a taxi to pick up the car from the pound. That was a very expensive outfit! We were issued a dark blue suit, white shirt, team tie, white Panama hat, and a red, white, and blue tracksuit.

Before I went to Barcelona some friends, Alison and Kenny Turnbull and Angela Moyes, made a special music tape for me to play in the call-up area before my races. It contained some of my favourite choruses, such as "Majesty" and "Servant King". There's a line in "Servant King" that says, "From Heaven you came, helpless babe." Mum says that was what I had been. No one dreamt that I would become a world-class athlete through determination, and yet here I was representing my country. Kenny had also included Queen's song "Barcelona". Little did I know at that stage that Queen and Freddie Mercury would be singing that at the opening ceremony.

On competition day we got up, had breakfast, and then went to warm up. Then we had to wait in the call-up area for forty-five minutes on our own. Although carers could be on hand, they were not allowed talk to you. As each race was called, you moved up a line until your race was at the front, the next to go. The call-up area can be very tense, and my tape was to give me encouragement. The Scottish competitors flew from Glasgow, and there was a lot of media attention, particularly from STV and the BBC. We were ushered outside in the rain for a group photo. Thankfully, we arrived in Barcelona to sunshine. At the games village we had to wait four hours for our accreditation. Then finally at one o'clock in the morning we were allocated an apartment. Mine was me and four other British swimmers, Paul Noble, Marc Woods, Adam Morley, and Phil Steadmond. Because of my snoring, I was given a room of my own.

We had a whale of a time. The village was near a beach, and we had a competition in the flat to see who could spot the girl with the biggest "frontage". We called it "snatch of the day", and Paul Noble bought a small Oscar for the daily winner to have. We all won it at various times. We ate in an underground food hall, and we had to use two long ramps to get to it. It was the first time I had a Magnum ice cream. It was all free and always available. I had two Magnums a day after that. In those days diet was not quite so important. The village was the first time I felt that the whole world was populated by disabled people. It felt very strange. There were just a few able-bodied carers and coaches, but they were outnumbered. Mum and Dad had come out. Friends and family had to meet us off-site because they were not allowed into the village. It was good to see them, but we athletes couldn't wait to get back to all the fun. It was a whole new experience for us. Little did I realise that four years later in Atlanta, competitors would be desperate to see their loved ones.

Our apartments were set round a central square, and before we were bussed to the opening ceremony we had to gather in the square for yet another team photo. We had to wait outside the stadium for four hours but were supplied with a picnic tea to keep us going. The ceremony in Barcelona had excellent music, with Freddie Mercury and Queen as well as opera. There were also huge papier-mâché figures moving around the teams, a great spectacle.

What a feeling walking into my first Paralympics opening ceremony. We were all spruced up in our national kit, and Team GB had Panama hats on. Coming out of the tunnel and into the arena, the hairs were standing up on the back of my neck. It was so exciting. Jim Thomson came to me and said, "Enjoy this. It might be your only one," and I really thought it would be. Even yet when I hear someone singing "Barcelona", I get butterflies in my stomach and the memories flood back.

Mum and Dad didn't get back to their hotel after the opening ceremony. An accident held up the train they were on, and all other trains had left. The station was closing, and a taxi driver quoted funny money to take them back. Mum and Dad said no thanks and spent the night on a park bench with only a Union Jack to keep them warm till morning – no cardigan, no jacket, only the national flag.

The pool in Barcelona was outdoors and built high up on a hill. Competitors were bussed up, but spectators either climbed up the hill or used the three escalators provided. These escalators all went upwards at the start of competition and were reversed at the end of the day. There were "dancing fountains" beautifully lit at the bottom of the hill and more water displays at the top.

I won my first silver medal at Barcelona. Peter Hull won gold, and Alan McGregor won bronze, a GB clean sweep. When the three Union Jacks went up together at the medal presentations, the atmosphere was amazing, and this result was repeated in two other races; what a feeling! Our medals were presented by Queen Sofia of Spain. I didn't realise who she was at the time, but Mum told me later. As it turned out, Peter Hull was reclassified to S3 a year later, and all his S2 world records were deleted. They decided that my times would stand, and I gained a whole lot of world records without any extra effort!

Before competition swimmers shave down to remove body, arm, and leg hair to make it easier to cut through the water, "shaving" milliseconds off their times. At that time I didn't shave down because my times were good enough. However, my four flatmates all did, and I called them all "wusses". I came back one day when Paul was shaving Marc's head, and they threatened to shave my eyebrows off. However, later in my career I learned to shave down as well.

I got a big fright one morning in Barcelona There were people going through the streets firing guns and shouting. I called through to Marc Woods that there was a world war starting. Marc said, "Go back to bed, Jim. It's only Catalonia Day." I just went back to bed! On our last night we had a big party that went on all night. There was a lot of celebrating. We all went to the closing ceremony, and that too was spectacular.

When we came back from Barcelona I was presented with lots of awards. West Lothian Council laid on a reception for me and Stephen Paton, a disabled runner. My picture in my swimming trunks had been taken beforehand and put up on the wall. It was very large and quite a scary sight, but we took it to Ferm Gran anyway. Every night she would look at it and say "Night, Jim." She said it kept her company! After Barcelona the Edinburgh and District Ladies Licensed Trade Auxiliary Association gave a cheque for the Paralympics at a dinner. Stephen Paton, Jim Thomson, and I were the only men in a room full of women as we collected it. Now that's brave! They also presented Stephen and me with quaichs as mementos. Various organisations asked me to speak as well. My speech is not always clear, but my friend Kenny Turnbull took me to these meetings and acted as my "interpreter".

Later that year we put on *Joseph* at my church. Dad played Jacob and Potiphar's wife and had some very quick costume changes! Mum, Ina Greenock, and Jean Turnbull played the backing group, "the Popettes", with Lindsay Williamson playing Pharaoh as Elvis in my disco-dancing outfit. I felt it was a great ending to my year. The fellowship was great, and I had made lots of new friends.

In December I was invited to BBC Scotland for a recording of *Sportscene*, Review of the Year, hosted by Dougie Donnelly and Hazel Irvine. That was a great night. At the reception after the recording, I first met Eddie McCluskey, a right gallus Glaswegian. He had been in Madrid at the Learning Disabilities Games while we were in Barcelona, and our paths hadn't crossed. Eddie rounded up people at the reception to come and speak to the Paralympics table: Alex Ferguson, Ally McCoist, Gavin Hastings, Steven Hendry, and many others.

That Christmas we were sent a glossy magazine of the Barcelona Paralympics, and among the photos was one of the crowd at the opening ceremony. There in the middle, resplendent in a big hat, was my mother.

In March 1993 I was awarded the WestLothiana sports award. Dorothy Paul, a popular Scottish actress, presented it to me at a meal in Howden House in Livingston. I got her autograph as an extra memento, and a video was made where the Scottish rugby team, led by Gavin Hastings, gave messages of congratulations.

In May of 1993 we had more family excitement when my second niece, Judith, was born. In June we went to Darlington for the National BSAD (British Sports Association for Disabled) Short-Course Championships. I won five gold medals and had my first-ever drug test. I nearly missed my evening meal because it took so long to produce a urine sample. I was called at 4 p.m. and didn't get away till about 8.30 p.m. I had to drink about five cartons of orange juice before they could get what they wanted. It was quite an experience. How do they expect sports people to give a sample quickly when they have been exerting themselves in competition?

Scotland won those championships regularly because we had people with a variety of disabilities on the team in those days. In August 1993 we had the Cerebral Palsy (CP) World Championships at Nottingham. We stayed in a nearby hotel for those games. I went to four CP World Championships, three in Nottingham and one in Connecticut. At my first I won every race I entered and established world records too. While I was in Nottingham for those first championships, Mum and Dad started building a conservatory on the back of our house. They had built the foundations and left it for a week while they came down to see me swim. When we got back they started building the walls, and every night their work was covered with a tarpaulin. One day Mum was taking the washing out. It had been raining heavily overnight, and all the water came off the cover and soaked her and the washing. It took two months to build.

In October we started the BSAD long-course championships in Sheffield. Before the end of my swimming career, I had taken part in twenty long-course championships. Peter Hull won gold, and I won silver at that first event, although Peter was reclassified into a higher class by the next year.

In October 1994 we had World Championships in Malta, run by the International Paralympic Committee. Qualification for these was again at Darlington. When we arrived in Malta it was quite alarming. It was Saturday night, and we were all in a bus going to our hotel. The bus could hardly get through the crowds going to a local nightclub. Mum and Dad came over to spectate and couldn't get over the state of the old buses. The opening ceremony had loads of balloons and a firework display. Those fireworks were very close to the competitors and caused a lot of alarm. The Royal Marines Band also played at the ceremony, a taste of home. These Malta games were the first World Championships held under IPC rules.

The event itself was held in a new outdoor pool. The pool area, including the car park, was a very muddy building site, very difficult for people in wheelchairs to get about. We went for our first training session in the pool before the competition. It was so hot, even at seven o'clock in the morning, and there was no shelter. However, one day, before the competition started, the weather changed and it rained so hard that the finals couldn't be held because the pool filled up too much. Our times in the heats were used for final placings. It's a lesson for everybody that they should swim fast in heats to get a good time or a favourable lane draw because you don't know what can happen. I won two golds and a silver medal. The competitor who beat me into silver had actually been put in the wrong class and was later moved into a higher classification for other races. He was allowed to keep his gold, but I got the times. Despite the weather, we had a fabulous time in Malta. On our last night we went to a bar with a karaoke machine. I had two of the female coaches, Morag and Jenny, sitting on my knee. I can't sing, but they made up for it.

The next summer, 1995, we booked a holiday in a caravan at York. I came home from New Trinity Centre and was walking into the house with my mum. I shouted, "Yippee, I'm on holiday," and promptly fell. I damaged my ankle and ended up at St John's Hospital in Livingston. Instead of two weeks in York, I ended up with two weeks on the living room floor, as I couldn't weight bear. My name was mud! Mum says now that anytime we're going on holiday, I'm not to open my mouth.

In 1995 we had European Championships in Perpignan, France. I remember that our hotel was on a roundabout and the food was so awful that we ate in a McDonalds. The indoor pool was so crowded that when we weren't swimming, they opened up the glass wall on one side of the pool and we had to sit outside. There just wasn't enough space poolside. I shared with Paul Noble at that event, and I kept him awake with my snoring. That was the last time I was allowed to share with a swimmer.

Atlanta 1996

Before the Atlanta games we were given a six-month window to achieve the qualifying time. We had a training camp with time trials in Sheffield, but it was snowing. The hotel was at the top of a hill and the pool was at the bottom. Imagine pushing us around in snow. The camp had to be closed early because of the weather! I achieved my times in March and April at the Olympic trials, and this was the first time they insisted we qualified in a 50-metre pool. We stayed about 5 miles out of Sheffield and travelled in daily by tram. We had training camps in Darlington every two months in the lead-up to Atlanta, and again our kit was issued at Stoke Mandeville.

In May before Atlanta we Scots competitors were all shocked. Pat Bennett, head of British Swimming, organised a training camp in Scotland (the first and only time). It was based at the Commonwealth Pool in Edinburgh. Despite living so close, I was expected to stay at the Edinburgh Airport Hotel. It had its compensation though, as I was given a room designed for people with disabilities. I was fascinated by the push-button operation of the curtains and the television, more than I was used to at home.

The Atlanta Paralympics in 1996 were, I'm afraid, my least favourite games. Our holding camp before the games was in a naval base in Pensacola, Florida. We flew into Atlanta and then had a six-hour bus journey to Pensacola, arriving at three in the morning. We couldn't go out at the base because we would have been eaten alive by mosquitos. All the dining facilities were at the top of a hill, and we shared it with US naval personnel, though what they thought of us I don't know. The pool we used was off base about fifteen minutes away by bus. We were allowed some use of a public pool, swimming widths rather than lengths, although the pool was 50 metres. The British Paralympic competitors were all made freemen of Pensacola, and I have the certificate to prove it. We were there for ten days before moving to Atlanta, and the excitement was building. But after all the great expectations there was a huge disappointment.

What a let-down; conditions in the village there were awful. Tom Scott, my carer in Malta, Barcelona, and Atlanta, had to do without a pillow for three days. In our flat in Atlanta Ian Gowans gave Kenny Cairns and me a row because we had told him Atlanta would be special. We had been to Barcelona and presumed Atlanta would be even better. It was Ian's first Paralympics, Kenny's third, and my second. The Olympics was run by one committee and the Paralympics by another. It was a nightmare. The Olympic Committee had sold off furniture, televisions, microwaves, and anything else they could raise money on, so when we arrived conditions were pretty basic. We had also been told there would be a bowling alley and cinema, but these had been trashed by the Olympic athletes on their last night.

When we all arrived and got our apartments, we discovered that the four bedrooms were kitted out with bunk beds, not very user-friendly for disabled athletes; no push-buttons here! Our coaches went round dismantling the bunks to make them both floor level. That's when I discovered my room was too small to get my wheelchair in. Our flat still had a microwave in it, but when we opened it there was a meal still inside from the Olympics two weeks beforehand. The plumbing was also suspect, and every time I flushed the toilet it broke. Most toilets had a stained carpet in front because they would regularly flood. We called it the Scottish flat. There were seven Scots and one long-suffering Englishman.

We decided that we should go together for our evening meal to the food hall. That turned out to be a marquee on top of a multistorey car park, and to get there, there was a mini-train, really just a small tractor with some trailers on the back. Some of the basketball players used to hang on the back and were towed up in their wheelchairs. We had to wait two hours for a meal because they ran out of food. Meals were all higgledy-piggeldy like a back-to-front buffet. The meal would arrive in instalments. It was a mess. The games site was on a hill, and accommodation was on a university campus, no specially built athletes' village. The competitors were all bored because there was nothing to do and nowhere to go between training and races. I personally couldn't go anywhere because the site was so hilly. The British team was invited to a reception by the British Ambassador, but after waiting five hours for our bus to arrive to take us, very few of us actually went. My mum and dad had come out for a holiday, but their holiday didn't really happen because they had to take me out and feed me. Normally families are kept separate from competitors, but not in Atlanta! British Airways and Royal Mail had done a lot of fundraising for the Paralympics and provided a hospitality area to sit with teas, coffees, and juice, and a television just for the British team.

We were bussed to the opening ceremony and were held in a baseball stadium for hours. At the ceremony there was a sea of Union Jacks, but my dad had a dishtowel with a saltire on it. The music at the opening ceremony was wonderful, but the speeches fell apart. Christopher Reeve, the actor who played Superman but who now had a serious spinal injury and was on a ventilator, was expected to deliver the opening speech. He really struggled. It felt a bit like the Americans were patronising us "poor disabled people" by bringing out one of their own.

Atlanta was the first time I was asked for my autograph. I had won a gold medal and got to meet Mum and Dad for a few minutes after the medal ceremony. A member of the public just came up and asked for my signature.

Our outfit for Atlanta was a striped blazer, cream trousers, a large yellow tie, and that panama hat. We looked like ice-cream salesmen. We were also issued tracksuits. Mine, by mistake, was the only one with Olympic rings instead of IPC teardrops.

The pool was horrible, again outdoors, and we had to get there up three long ramps. There was regular thunder and lightning, and Mum and Dad were sitting in the stands on metal seats. The spectators were told it was safe, as the seats were earthed. The stands had a solid roof with canvas drop-down walls that were supposed to protect those watching. The wind just drove the rain into the stand, and everyone was drenched to the skin. It became obvious that this was anticipated, as the local Red Cross had piles of towels for people to dry themselves. Swimming had to stop until the storms passed. I won two golds and a silver medal. The Polish swimmer who beat me to that third gold thanked me, as his gold medal meant he would now be given a car when he got home. Between races our women coaches tried to lighten the atmosphere by dancing the Macarena!

One night someone said, "If there was a plane available, would we all like to go home?" Everyone, staff, competitors, and families all said yes. We were all so fed up by the end of the games that we boycotted the closing and went to a pub instead. We arrived back in London from the games at five o'clock in the morning and were given a breakfast reception at Heathrow. Afterwards we had to hang about the airport till our homeward flight at four in the afternoon, just pleased to be back in the UK.

Again when we got back, West Lothian Council held a reception in Livingston for Stephen and me, and this time they gave us gold watches. In December there was a reception for Olympians and Paralympians in the great hall of Edinburgh Castle, a huge room that has a very high ceiling and is very cold! Later that month the Paralympians were invited to BBC Sports Personality of the Year in London. I wasn't feeling particularly well, and of all things it turned out I had chickenpox! But after the Atlanta games I also made it into the *Guinness Book of World Records* as the fastest very severely disabled swimmer in 100-metre freestyle, with a time of 2 minutes, 41.94 seconds. John Major invited me was invited and the Paralympic team to 10 Downing Street. He was very welcoming to us all and said we could just wander round all the rooms. I remember lots of display cases. I wandered into the dining room, and the table was all set out with silver. It's a great feeling walking down Downing Street and going into number ten.

In 1997 I visited Buckingham Palace for the first time. Mum came with me and helped me up the stairs. It was a reception celebrating "sport in the life of the nation". All sorts of sports people were there, and there were lots of recognisable faces. When we came away from the palace and down some steps, Chris Eubank, the boxer, and one of the soldiers just picked me up in my chair and carried me down to the bottom.

Also in 1997 British Swimming took over from Sport England, and National Lottery money came on board for the first time. Before that swimming was more relaxed and fun, but now it became more of a "proper" job, with proper training. You also had to have a "proper" coach. Mine was Don McFarlane. Swimming was more professional, as you had to meet the criteria for times to remain part of the squad; that is, earn your money or you're out. There was a lot of controversy because British Swimming had new ideas. Change is never easy, and there were tensions in the management of the team because of the changes. Accommodation at events also changed. We had European Championships in Bandajoz, Spain. It was a bit like an up-market holiday resort, with an outdoor pool surrounded by grass and plants. There was a wedding in the hotel, and the hotel staff wanted us to stay in our rooms during it, so they put free "adult" movies on our televisions. I was sharing a room, and needless to say, we both enjoyed the entertainment.

That year we also had CP World Championships in Nottingham, where we stayed on the university campus. We were swimming for Scotland in those games. Scotland was one of the original members of the Cerebral Palsy International Sports and Recreation Association and was allowed to compete as a separate nation. We travelled down by bus, and the multisport games lasted ten days. I slept on the floor because the bed was too narrow and my shoulders were built up by my swimming. I kept rolling out of the bed, so my mattress was put on the floor for comfort and safety. We ate on campus, but the meals were a bit like school dinners, although we did have a choice of meals. Staff brought them to us on trays.

It was a hot summer, and I spent some time sitting outside my room enjoying the sunshine. The programme for the swimming competition had been made up and was on a computer. One of the officials, Jill Stidever, went to print it out but hit the wrong button and wiped it instead. The World Championship gala was delayed for an hour while it was rewritten. We had lots of fun with discos and karaoke in the evenings. I won all my races there and broke CP world records.

In June 1998 everything was going well, but one Friday night in a matter of minutes our whole family world was turned upside down. I came home from Trinity singing and laughing, but Mum had news for me. Dad had had a bad accident and suffered a serious head injury. I had to grow up very quickly; one day a typical disabled person without a care in the world, and the next a proper grown-up person with responsibilities. It was hard. Dad was in the Western General Hospital, Edinburgh in an induced coma. I had to help Mum and talk to doctors and nurses. One of the doctors thought I was the patient and not my dad. I had to become the man of the house. In many ways I became even closer to Mum because for a change, I had to support her through that time, when we were both so worried about Dad. Mum's attitude is to share the good and the bad in life; just because you have a disability, you shouldn't be sheltered from dark times. At the time we weren't sure Dad was going to make it through the first weekend. One evening, coming home from the hospital, Mum said, "Everything is going to be all right!" There was a beautiful rainbow over the house, the sign of hope, and gradually Dad regained his health. He still has no memory of the two weeks and two days after the accident and sometimes has difficulty remembering words, but he is still with us.

We had a lot of training camps in America in 1998. In August after the Atlanta games we went to Florida and stayed in a wonderful apartment block. Our meals were next door at a private hospital. There were difficult moments at that time because the more able Paralympic swimmers felt that those of us in wheelchairs were holding them back at training camp. That's when we got able-bodied swim coaches on board who knew nothing of disability. We organised a disability awareness course for them. I thought at that time that the less able were treated as though we were not elite athletes, despite having been selected for the camps like all the others. It was not a happy time.

But in 1998 I discovered my favourite place for the first time. The IPC World Championships were to be in Christchurch, New Zealand, and our holding camp was on Queensland's Gold Coast in Australia. The Gold Coast is beautiful, and on our day off we went down to the beach, where I went paddling. I suddenly realised that I was paddling in the Pacific Ocean; imagine wee me from Broxburn paddling in this vast ocean so far from home!

We flew to New Zealand for the competition and swam in the 1960 Commonwealth Games pool in Christchurch. I went for a walk around Christchurch, and it was like being in a Western movie. The houses all seemed to be wooden with verandas. In Christchurch we stayed in a hotel but ate in the corridor of Parliament House. The opening ceremony was held in Victoria Park, where squirrels were everywhere. There were the usual speeches and then Maori singing and dancing. The Maoris challenged us with the Hakka, and it was the first time I had seen all their culture and national dress. A few of the locals watched the ceremony! I went to church one day in New Zealand. It was very bright inside, and I was upset when many years later the building was all but destroyed by an earthquake.

It's daft but I felt upside down in New Zealand, and this was the first time I had swum 200 metres in competition. Before New Zealand they said that S2 swimmers couldn't swim 200 metres, and this was the first event to include it in the race schedule for IPC World Championships. Because I won that race, I became the first-ever world record holder for S2 200-metre freestyle, breaking my 50-metre time and my 100-metre time on the way to winning. I won three golds and a silver at that event.

I liked it so much on the Gold Coast that I was desperate to go back, and I have now been six times: in 1998 on the way to New Zealand, twice in 1999, twice in 2000, and once in 2008. My carer wasn't able to come on my second visit to Australia, so I got a new carer, Paul McInneny, through New Trinity. I told him there was one condition: he would have to give up smoking. Funny enough, he couldn't swim. And it was on the Gold Coast that Paul finally learnt, at the age of twenty-eight. On the Gold Coast we stayed in a Radisson Hotel next to a golf course. The rooms were motel types and set round a pool. Meals were served in the main hotel building. We trained in an outdoor 50-metre pool at a local girls' school, St Hilda's, which an English lady set up in 1924. This lady had shipped out all the furniture and fittings from England, in real colonial fashion.

The setting was wonderful, and I felt like a king. One night we were lying on our beds in the hotel and wanted to change TV channels. I couldn't manage it, so I threw the remote control to Paul and burst his nose – but we're still speaking. We used to have a coffee club. Some of us would meet up for a coffee at night and would sit and watch the world go by. We took turns to buy the coffees, Tim Reddish, Pippa the team manager, Spencer Moore, Paul McInneny, and myself.

At the girls' school there was a sponge pool, a kind of soft play area. My colleagues used to throw me in there, and I couldn't get out. We had lots of fun times. I went three times one year from Scotland to the same Radisson, and lottery money meant I could employ someone to go with me. In 1999 I was number one in the world, and my two visits were in January and October. It was funny being in hot weather in January on Burns Night; most peculiar. My favourite part was waking up at 5.45 a.m. with sun beating into our rooms. It was fun watching Paul walking up for breakfast in T-shirt and shorts at 6.45 a.m. We went in buses to St Hilda's for training and arrived in time to hear the school bell ringing and see the girls going into class while we went to the pool. Jill Stidever and Eddie were my coaches. We did our warm-ups and then got into the water for more work. Paul and Eddie were lifting me out of the water one day and both ended up in the water with me because they slipped on the edge.

We had been warned always to look out for red-backed spiders. One day I needed to go to the toilet and was sitting there when a very large tarantula-type spider started climbing up the wall beside me. I let out a scream, and Eddie came running to see what the matter was. He yelled, and the janitor came running with a fire extinguisher. The janitor hit the spider with it but didn't kill it, and it fell between my feet. There was no need for laxatives that day!

In May 1999 we went to Braunschweig, Germany, for the German Open Championships for Disabled People. Held in a 50-metre pool, those championships were a nightmare. On the Saturday my first race was at about 8 a.m. and my last was at 8.45 at night. We left the hotel at 6 a.m. and got back at 11 p.m. An athlete's life is not all glamour. We stayed in a hotel where we didn't get much sleep, as it was next to a busy railway station. The food was poor, and we ended up buying snacks at the station. We walked to the venue through a grassy park, full of rabbits. I went back to Braunschweig in August for the European Championships. I managed to get four world records at that event. My fourth medal was put round my neck, but later that night I couldn't find it. Paul Mac went haywire looking for it. We went all over and through the park, back to the pool, and everywhere. It was the first time Paul Mac had been at a major competition with me, and he was worried he wouldn't be allowed back. He went to the organisers and arranged for another medal for me. Later that night we went back to our room, and when I went through to the toilet, there was a thump on the bathroom floor. And there was my medal. It must have slipped down inside my shirt and into my trousers; relief all round! In celebration we shared a bottle of champagne!

I was never at home that year, as I went back out to Australia in October. There was a Paralympic competition called the Southern Cross Games where we tested out the pool in Sydney in preparation for the full Paralympics in 2000. When I went into the Olympic pool I gasped. I couldn't get over the size of the venue. Previous Olympic pools were outdoors, but the Sydney one was in a very bright building with rows and rows of seats going right up to the roof. It was like a different world. There were ten lanes in the main pool, and we sat near the diving pool waiting to compete. The Southern Cross Games were the games where I found I had my trunks on inside out and I had to be taken away quickly to put them on properly and rush back to the starting blocks.

    Sydney is a beautiful city built on hills round a natural harbour. By the harbour there are many, many restaurants of all types. Sydney became the place where we ate in a different restaurant every night. From our hotel I saw the Sydney Opera House for the first time and couldn't get over the size of it. I said to myself, "Yes, I've made it." We went out in minibuses over Sydney Harbour Bridge. Jill was driving ours and thought she was following Eddie, who was driving the other one. We ended up in a housing scheme though because Jill had been following a painter and decorator's van. We were all in fits of laughter. There's a wonderful marine aquarium where we spent hours watching the sea life going by in a very deep glass-sided tank. The weather in Sydney was so warm we could go around in T-shirts at ten o'clock at night.

Sydney 2000

We had a training camp prior to Sydney in January on the Gold Coast for both Olympic and Paralympic Teams. It was for warm weather training; two weeks of swimming and sun-bathing in my favourite hotel; Paradise! There was a gym at the hotel, and Paul McInneny and I went to use the static bikes in the afternoons. We were working one day when the rowers came in: Steve Redgrave, Matthew Pinsent, and James Cracknell. I was so excited to be in such company, but Paul felt tiny beside them.

In 2000 we did a lot of competitions in Europe. At that time I was number one in the world. Later in January we went to Castres in France, and it felt bitterly cold after Australia. We stayed in a motel where the door opened directly to the outside. In the morning I couldn't believe how deep the snow was. There was deep snow everywhere, and I don't know how Paul McInneny was able to push me around. We were bussed to the pool, but I felt cold all day. I was beaten then, so early in the season. It was a Frenchman, Phillipe Revillon, who beat me, but he got his qualification time for the Paralympics. I didn't but didn't worry too much because I knew I had other chances.

In March we went to Denmark, and it was cold. I swam well. We stayed in the Danish Institute of Sport. I was amazed at the size of the multisport complex. Come April, it was back to the Gold Coast with the whole Paralympic Team for another training camp. There was a team doctor, Dr Nick Webber, who was into acupuncture. That was the first and last time I tried it. Never again! Lots of needles in my back, and it didn't help my arthritis.

In May we had our own national gala in Sheffield, and that's where I qualified for my third Paralympics, in three events. It was easy for me in those days. I just had to get in the water and swim. Further on in May we went to Turka in Finland, and what a gorgeous place we stayed in. The hotel was built beside a lake, and it never got dark. It was odd because it looked like summer but was cold. The restaurant was built on stilts over the lake and had beautiful views.

On the Saturday evening, after a good swim, we walked round the lake. Later in 2000 on the Sunday afternoon after competition in Berlin, we were taken on a minibus tour of the city. They showed us the 1936 Olympic stadium, where Hitler wanted Germany to win everything. I found it all very creepy. The swimming pool for the competition was built in a bunker, with pools on two levels. I managed to miss a race because I was in the upstairs warm-up pool and should have been downstairs racing. Kenny Cairns had discovered that the diving boards were accessed by lift. We looked up to see Kenny pushing himself in his wheelchair to the edge of the top board as if he was going to dive in. We were all very relieved when he turned back to the lift and came down the slow way.

A swimmers' team-building event in Vichy, France, was next, where we stayed in a sports complex used by Arsenal F.C. for their preseason preparations. In the evenings some of the competitors and staff played tennis. I remember it being very hot and dry. They used to do daily urine tests on us to check our hydration levels, but the test machine broke down. It took two days for Eddie and Spencer to fix it, and we were very pleased not to have to provide samples. It also meant we could get a long lie on those two days. Eddie, a telecoms engineer, went into the town and managed to find a part in a domestic appliance shop. I don't know how his "French" translated, but Eddie can talk his way through anything.

Before the Paralympics in October we went to the Gold Coast for ten days' preparation. The whole Paralympic team was there, and our outfit was a navy blue suit, a white shirt, and a narrow tie with the

IPC teardrops on it. We flew down to Sydney and into the Olympic village, where I shared with my friend Kenny Cairns. It was back to a proper Paralympic village after Atlanta with a massive food hall. It's my opinion that every village since has been modelled on Sydney. The British High Commissioner invited the British team to a reception before the games. We travelled by boat through the spectacular harbour area and were bussed back afterwards. It was a very hot day, but we had to be in our suits and ties. Maggie McEleny, a Scottish swimmer, carried the Team GB flag at the opening ceremony. She was pushed by her coach, the same Eddie McCluskey. We also had a huge panoramic team photo taken, like those pictures of the whole military college or police graduations.

Sydney was the first Paralympics with large crowds. The Aussies really like their sport. It was so noisy I couldn't hear the person next to me speaking. I went into the competition big-headed, thinking *I'm the best*. I got the biggest slap in the face. I was beaten in backstroke by someone wrongly classified (Malta all over again). He was reclassified an hour later but was allowed to keep the gold medal he had already been presented with. What put the tin lid on it was that the man who presented the medals was David McRae, a Scot I knew well. As he put the silver medal round my neck, he whispered in my ear, "We all know it should have been gold." I found I had tears running down my face when he said that. The same thing happened to my friend Kenny in his classification. British Swimming went to the Court of Arbitration for Sport but didn't win their appeal. My next race included Curtis Lovejoy, an American ex-soldier paralysed from the neck down in an accident. He was great in freestyle, doing everything in front crawl. I was doing about one minute, twelve for 50 metres, and Curtis went out and did it in one minute flat. My carer Paul Mac and my coach Jill just stood with their mouths open in disbelief. When I got out of the water Jill and I just burst into tears of disappointment. I was number one but well beaten on the day. The same thing happened in the 100 metre. Curtis beat me again. I ended up with three silvers in Sydney and was very disappointed. I felt so low. I couldn't wait to get home. I was emotionally drained. But when I got home I threw myself back into training.

In Sydney my friend had cut my hair, or rather, had shaved my head. Mum went mental when she met me. She had seen the effect on television and says my head is the wrong shape to be shaved. Our last night in Sydney, we had been out celebrating and I managed to fall in a pub toilet. One of the team helpers came to rescue me but couldn't get me up. Eventually, after lots of giggling, we managed to get up and return to the party. On our return from Sydney, the Scottish Olympians and Paralympians were invited to a reception at Edinburgh Castle, and we met First Minister Jack McConnell for the first time.

In January 2001 I went to Florida for a training camp. When we got there, there had been major forest fires, and for ten days on our way to and from the pool we could smell smoke. I did my normal training in the mornings. In the afternoon Jill had me trying breast stroke, but I never mastered it. We had a day off and visited Warner Brothers theme park. There were lots of rides, and I would have gone on lots of them but my carer chickened out. I had a caricature portrait made though, as a souvenir. On the bus ride back to the hotel, an "old dearie" spoke to my carer, saying, "You have a heart of gold taking this poor boy away on holiday. You must be a very special person." I just bit my tongue! Little did she know this was no holiday. Our flight home was eventful because a passenger was taken ill and we were diverted to Nova Scotia. We had a five-hour delay while the plane was de-iced before we set off again.

There was a reception at Buckingham Palace for Olympians and Paralympians with the Queen and Prince Philip. We also met the Countess of Wessex and Duchess of Gloucester. In the palace Mum and I had a good look round because we thought this would be our one and only visit. In the green room were wall cabinets full of china and large ornate vases, all with a green theme, funny enough. The music room was decorated in gold and had fascinating instruments, some beautifully painted. After the reception, we left the palace. It was Valentine's Day 2001 after dark, and there wasn't a taxi to be had. We walked through Green Park to get a cab from the other side. It was very creepy because people were already sleeping on benches; palace to park bench in a short walk! As I could only take one guest, Dad had stayed behind at the hotel and was all dressed up, ready to go out for a Valentine's dinner when we got back.

There was a training camp in Manchester, and at the same time there were CP World Championships at Nottingham. We were allowed to compete at Nottingham for one day only. We got up at 4.30 a.m., but there were no staff members up. How were we to get our breakfast? Eddie got into the kitchen at the hotel and made breakfast for us. We left at 7 a.m., with Eddie driving the minibus. It took us three hours to get there over narrow winding roads through the Peak District. I was delighted to swim for Scotland and managed gold medals and a CP world record that day.

Between Sydney and Athens we went to Sweden for a weekend meet, the Swedish Open Championships, and were based beside a canal. In the evening we would go for a walk along the banks of the canal, and we spent ages watching the barges going through the locks. It was gorgeous. In 2001 the European Championships were in Stockholm. We also frequently went to competitions in Denmark.

At that time Scottish Swimming awards were presented annually in different places. Once at Carnoustie there was a muddle over bookings and some people were sent to other hotels. The Andersons, however, were put in a penthouse suite with a special security key for the lift. There were two huge bedrooms with king-size beds, and a sitting room with a large dining table, a massive TV, and windows over the beds so that you could stargaze all night if you wanted. One year the awards were in Aberdeen, and there was deep snow. We were met by snowmen! Two days later my parents took me back to Aberdeen to fly to Denmark, still with deep snow on the ground. We all stayed in an airport hotel overnight, and in the morning Mum, Dad, and six competitors all had breakfast together. One of the waitresses thought they were all Mum's children. What a family that would have been!

In 2002 the World Championships were in Argentina, an eight-hour flight to Buenos Aires and another eight-hour bus journey to get to Mar del Plata, the home port of the battleship *Belgrano*, sunk during the Falklands conflict. It was strange to have travelled so far and yet only have a one-hour time difference. After long journeys like that we were always taken to the pool for a loosening swim to help with travel weariness and stiffness. It was tough going but certainly helped.

The hotel was right on the seafront, and the food was excellent. When we got up in the morning, we could see all the fishing boats going out to fish. It made me think of Jim McLeod singing "Forty Shades of Green" and the line about "fishing boats in Dingle". There were sea lions on the beach. Behind the hotel though, there were crowded shanty towns of poverty-stricken people, easily seen as we were bussed to and from the pool. It was October and very hot. Paul McInneny and I went for a walk down to the harbour, and there were lots of people fishing off the pier. We had a chance to visit a gift shop and bought lots of stone tortoises as souvenirs.

The pool was built under a glass dome, and it was extremely hot inside. The organisers had erected a marquee inside the dome to try to provide some shade. The call-up area was in a corridor and was so narrow that two wheelchairs couldn't pass. I remember there weren't many spectators either. On the second-to-last day of competition, all the medals were stolen. They still held presentation ceremonies but had to "borrow" back medals awarded earlier in the week. It took months to get the right medals sent out to us. I won four gold medals at this event and was excited to be back as world number one, having beaten Curtis in the 50 metre and 100 metre. I broke my own 200-metre freestyle world record, but in all the years I swam I was never able to beat Curtis's Sydney 50-metre world record. It has since been beaten by a Chinese swimmer.

One laugh we did have in Mar del Plata was at the expense of Jill Stidever. At the end of each race coaches would grab the arm of the competitor to pull them out of the water. Not every pool has suitable access for people with disabilities. Jill grabbed Maggie McEleny's arm but overbalanced and ended up in the pool herself. Luckily Jill is a giggler and saw the funny side.

In 2003 a group of us went to an open meet in Canada for ten days. At that time British competitors were sent to different places depending where our nearest rivals were competing. Curtis found it a short trip up from the States. I swam well but broke no records winning my medals.

At Easter 2003 I was back in America for a camp, where I first met Paul Martin. It was also the first time I visited Disney World. That was an experience and a half. There was a huge car park, and we had to get a boat over to the island where the theme park is. Round the outside of the car park were dozens of hotels with excited, noisy people filling every space.

That year we also had a British Paralympic team training camp in Cyprus and used an outdoor pool. On our day off Paul Mac and I went up the highest building on the island by lift and looked over to the Turkish side from Nicosia. The building was in a pedestrianized shopping area, and Woolworths occupied the ground floor. At the top of the street was a high wall with soldiers on guard on top, marking the separation of the island between the Turkish north and Greek south. There is a house in Nicosia that was abandoned when Cyprus was divided. The lady who lived there just left everything behind. We passed that house every day going to the pool. I was a bit disappointed that we couldn't go out and about there in wheelchairs. Cyprus is the worst place for accessibility. Its old towns have narrow streets with either no pavements or very narrow ones, built well before cars came into use. Paul Mac and I did manage to go out for a walk one day to go to a supermarket. The supermarket already had official Olympic and Paralympic merchandise for sale, and excitement was certainly building. We met Paul Martin halfway, and he bought a tube of Pringles. I was on a diet. Because the streets were narrow and it was difficult for me to get around, I told Paul Mac to just go on. I would stay and blether to Paul Martin. Needless to say, Paul Martin and I ate the Pringles on the quiet, with no one any the wiser. At night we were sitting round a table having our evening meal, and

Paul Mac admitted he had had a packet of crisps in the supermarket without telling us. Paul Martin and I just burst out laughing. We laughed so much we couldn't finish our meal. We couldn't explain what was so funny.

At that time, after my arthritic illness, I was petrified to lie on my stomach. Paul Martin is a physio, and one day at the gym he told me to get on my stomach. I told Paul I couldn't do it, but he insisted and massaged my back until I was able to lie flat. I then couldn't get back up, and Paul had to help me back into my wheelchair again. My usual physio in Stirling and I had many laughs. She threatened that if I didn't do what I was told, the physio fairy would haunt me. I must have done it right because I haven't seen the fairy yet. I used to go to physio in Stirling, and the receptionist, Elaine Allison, had a fairy wand behind her desk. Every time I went to a competition she had a ritual of sprinkling me with magic fairy dust. If I was in three races, she would wave the wand over me three times. The wand had a battery in it and made a "fairy" noise. I also had to touch her desk. It was all supposed to bring me luck. She was happy because she thought it worked.

A sign of things to come; my brother Stuart
(l) and me enjoying the water

My BBC Scotland Sports Personality of 2004 award

With two of the Pauls who have put up with me over the years, Mac (l) and Martin

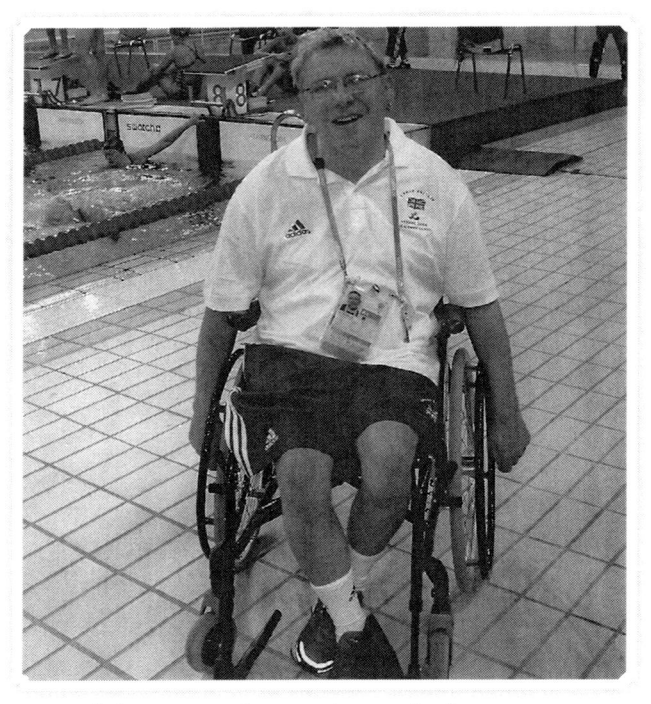

A bigger pool, warming up before a race

Presentation of my story writing prize 1997

More prizes, one of my medals and laurel
wreaths from the Athens games

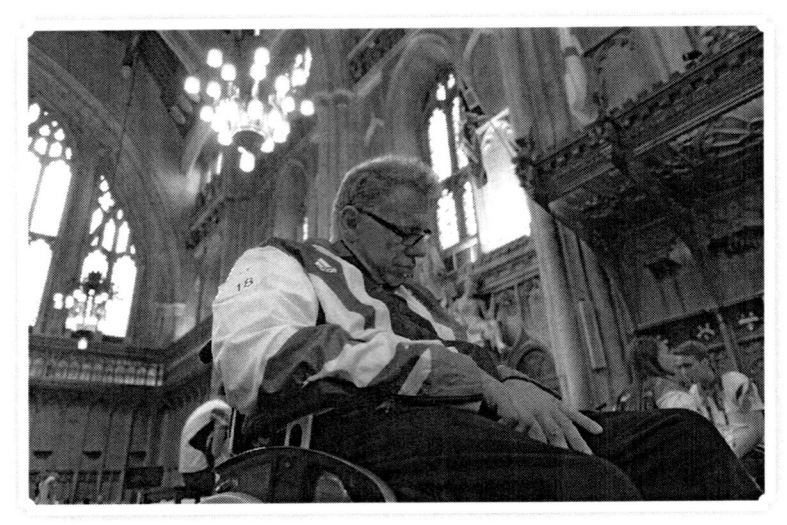

The morning after the night before! asleep in the Mansion House after the closing of the London games

At Buckingham Palace for the Investiture of my O.B.E. Cousin Anne at the back, Mum in blue and Dad and I in our Anderson tartan kilts

Athens 2004

I qualified for my fourth Paralympics at the Olympic and Paralympic trials in Sheffield in April 2004, breaking British, European, and world records at that meet. In July we went to Nottingham for a British Paralympic Association weekend where all the sports team members met up to hear all about the arrangements for Athens. We were also given our "Sunday best" uniforms.

Before moving on to a holding camp in Cyprus for the Athens Paralympics, we were asked to go to an able-bodied meet in Manchester. This gala was trials for the able-bodied short-course World Championships, which included races for disabled swimmers. We had previously been issued our sports kit for Athens at a training camp in Manchester. Paul Mac couldn't come down to that camp, so Mum and Dad came to collect me on the way back from their holiday. I had my training kit, my Olympic kit, and Paul's Olympic kit – two bags each! With all that, plus Mum and Dad's holiday bags, my wheelchair, and my walker, there wasn't room to move on the way home. However, when I arrived in Cyprus I found I had no kit. British Airways had managed to lose my bags. The bags turned up two days later, but meantime I had to borrow kit from the physio, Paul Martin, because he was the only one big enough. I had only what was in my backpack. It wasn't too bad though because I had one change of clothes and my swimming kit. We were always told to take our swimming kit in our hand luggage in case bags did go missing. We were also given T-shirts with London 2012 on them to help publicise the bid for the London Olympics. At the airport on our way to Athens, Paul McInneny bent down to fold up my footplates. I took a spasm and nearly knocked him out when I kicked him in the face.

Athens was where I had my most successful games. The Paralympic village was really spread out, and it seemed miles and miles to get anywhere. The British team was housed farthest away from the food hall. Because of numbers, Paul Mac and I ended up sharing a block with the weight-lifting competitors. One day I met Prince Edward in the food hall, and he amused me no end by saying, "When you all come back, Mummy is having a party at Buckingham Palace."

In Athens we were bussed from the village to the pools, which were built on the side of a hill. There were special Olympics lanes on the road to allow easy transit for officials and competitors. We had to use a lift to get to the pools. There were two: one outdoors for warm-ups where the physios were based and the other indoors for the competitions. There was another pool back at the village for all competitors to relax in. I came home with four gold medals, two world records, two of my four laurel wreaths, and some of the flowers from my winner's bouquets. I beat my own 200-metre world record by 12 seconds (4 minutes, 49.81 seconds). Everyone was amazed, including me. Paul Mac was sure I would come out of the water breathless and blue because I was swimming so fast. This was the first time this length of race was included in the Paralympics, after trying it at the World Championships in New Zealand in 1998.

At the second medal ceremony of the four, I got quite emotional because I was getting world records and Mum and Dad were at home and not sharing the occasion with me. I suddenly felt very homesick. My coach, Anthony Stickland, helped me to win those four medals, but all the press coverage said I "picked up four medals", as if I'd just found them lying about somewhere. Mum and Dad had been listening to commentary on BBC Radio 5 Live and heard my name mentioned just as they switched to a different event. They had to wait till much later to find out what had actually happened.

I got my nick-name of Jim the Swim in Athens. My friend Paul Noble was commentating and called me "Jim the Swim" as he was talking. Clare Balding picked it up and used it in her commentary, and it has stuck with me ever since. When we left Athens for home all the gold medallists were put at the front of the plane. We got off first at Heathrow and were taken to an airport hotel for a press conference. It was all very exciting. We were then ushered into a reception in the same hotel, another new experience. When I got back to Edinburgh a lot of my friends were at the airport to meet me with banners, balloons, and general celebration. On Sunday at church they had made me a cake and a "well done" certificate. I felt like some kind of superstar. A man in the Gyle Shopping Centre in Edinburgh even stopped to shake my hand! Auntie June was so proud of me that she organised an afternoon tea at her sheltered housing complex in St Andrews, just to show me off to her friends. I made the headlines in the St Andrews Citizen!

In September, two weeks after I got back, we went to London for a parade of Olympic and Paralympic medallists. At that time London was preparing for the bid for 2012, and the parade was part of the publicity for that bid. We got on a lorry at a hotel near Buckingham Palace and travelled through the streets of London to a big celebration on a stage in Trafalgar Square. There was a huge sense of celebration, with balloons and streamers, and office workers hanging out of windows. The able-bodied swimmer Steve Parry said with a laugh, "I'm not standing next to you with all that gold round your neck!" and moved down the lorry. Afterwards Mum, Dad, and I got in a taxi to go back to our hotel, and the cabbie refused to take any money because he had a Gold medallist in his cab.

The promised visit to "Mummy's party" in Buckingham Palace happened in October when ParalympicsGB went to an evening reception. All the gold medallists were ushered into a separate room, and the Queen spoke to each of us. She shook my hand and then shook my mother's hand. Mum was thrilled and went on to have a long chat with one of the ladies-in-waiting. Also in October 2004 Jack McConnell, then Scottish first minister, invited Scottish Olympians and Paralympians to Bute House, his official residence in Edinburgh, to celebrate our successes.

November was busy too. There was a Scottish Sports Aid Awards dinner at the Sheraton Hotel in Edinburgh, and the Paralympians were also invited to a Scottish autumn test rugby international at Murrayfield against Australia, with hospitality in the president's suite. We all paraded around the pitch before the match. We were also invited to the Getty art gallery in London to an exhibition of photographs of the Olympics and Paralympics. There was an almost life-size picture of me after one of the medal ceremonies, in tracksuit and bare feet and with a laurel wreath on my head. The photo was presented to me, but it was too big for the house. We gave it to Seonaid Airth, my physio, of Physiofocus Stirling. They had built an extension including a gymnasium, and I was invited to open it. To celebrate my Athens success, they had provided a huge cake, and I passed on my photo. The *gym* was renamed *Jim*.

Mum, Dad, and I felt we were living in London at that time. We went down to London on a Wednesday and had to go to Leeds on the Friday for another competition. The old Leeds pool was the worst pool ever. I hated it. The roof ran at the opposite angle to the pool, and swimming backstroke, I couldn't tell where in the length I was. I ended swimming to one side of my lane. We couldn't use the disabled toilets because they were full of boxes and were being used as storerooms. British Swimming insisted we swam there, and the pool has since been replaced.

I received many other awards. I was competing at the Welsh Open Championships, and my coach spoke to Mum and Dad early on Saturday morning. I was to go to the BBC Wales studios in Swansea at nine o'clock. All I could think was *What does the BBC want to speak to me for?* John Beattie phoned me from Glasgow to tell me I was BBC Scotland Sports Personality of the Year, the first disabled person to win it. I was on live radio and totally speechless. My parents had phoned Stuart, who recorded the programme for us, as it wasn't broadcast in Wales. I had beaten, among others, Colin Montgomerie and Chris Hoy that year. All day that Saturday I was going about with a big grin on my face. I knew I had been nominated, but I never, ever expected to win the award. I found out about my nomination because we were watching *Sportscene* one Saturday when the list of nominees came up with my face among them, not what you expect on a Saturday afternoon!

I competed on the Sunday morning in Wales and then got into Paul Martin's car and headed for London, leaving Mum and Dad behind. Mum was pleased because she got all her Christmas cards written while I was away. On the Sunday evening I was at BBC Television Centre in London for the British Sports Personality of the Year programme. Chris Hoy gave me my trophy in the corner of the room off camera. We Scots were not recognised! We went back to Wales on the Monday by minibus and travelled back to Scotland with Mum and Dad, in a bit of a daze.

I was also awarded the Sports Writers' Sports Personality of the Year, a big cup that was posted to me, as I was competing at the time of the prize-giving dinner. At home in West Lothian I won the Celebration of Sporting Excellence Award, and at the ceremony I had a wonderful surprise, an e-mail from my sporting hero David Wilkie congratulating me on my four golds. John Beattie was compère that evening, and my parents received a painting for their support of me in my sport.

I was awarded the MBE in the New Year honours list too. What a year that was. When the letter arrived in November asking me if I would accept the honour, I was competing in short-course championships in Sheffield. I didn't know about it till I got home, a lovely surprise. They announce the New Year's Honours list on 31 December each year, but on the 30th I had lots of phone calls from the press who had prior notice of the award winners. I was so excited to make it into the *Daily Record*, especially as they had never reported any of my past achievements, including my four Paralympic golds.

When I went to Buckingham Palace for the investiture, Mum, Dad, and Auntie Betty accompanied me. We went down to London two days before the investiture to do some sightseeing. When Mum booked the train tickets, Dad said she should book an extra seat for her hat box! On the first day, we went to Westminster Abbey, and I couldn't get over the length of the nave. We stayed at the Berners

Hotel, and as we had stayed there several times since the Athens games, we became well known to the maître d'. He was from Athens and wanted to give us a bottle of wine in celebration. We thanked him but explained we didn't drink wine. Somehow though we were not charged for our sweets at the meal!

Early next morning it was full English breakfast before getting into my kilt for the ceremony. When we were ready we went downstairs, and Mum said her favourite phrase: "Taxi for Buckingham Palace, please." When we got there Mum and Auntie Betty were shown to the ballroom, and Dad and I were taken the other way to be given our instructions with the other people receiving awards. We were advised on the protocols, etiquette, and procedures we would face. When it was my turn Dad pushed me up to where her Majesty was standing, and I was so excited and nervous that I bowed twice. After my investiture we were able to join Mum and Auntie Betty to watch the others. Spaces had been reserved for those of us with mobility difficulties. Auntie Betty ended up sitting next to Eric Sykes and was thrilled to bits. After all the ceremonies were finished we were all taken out to the courtyard to have photos taken. After the photos, I took my parents and Auntie Betty for a slap-up lunch. Our special day was topped off in the evening when we went to see *Chitty Chitty Bang Bang* at the London Palladium.

In March 2005 we went to the Danish Open championships, where we stayed in a hostel. The food was all home-made, and Jill, our coach, came home with all the recipes. One of the most exciting things that year was a VIP day at Wimbledon. The letter about it came when I was in Denmark. I was over the moon when Mum phoned to tell me. I told everybody over and over again I was going to Wimbledon, in my excitement. Eventually Derek Martin, the team doctor – the original Doc Martin – told me to shut up about it! We went down to London on the Wednesday beforehand. It was very hot and I had forgotten to pack a hat, so we had to go and buy one. On the way to Wimbledon on the Thursday, we drove past all the queues of people camping out for tickets and sailed straight into the All-England Club. I was surprised how compact Wimbledon is. We arrived about 10.30 a.m. and went round Henman Hill, the museum, and the beautiful grounds all planted out in the Wimbledon colours of purple and green. The Paralympians all met up and went for lunch hosted by Ann Jones. We had complementary tickets for No. 1 Court. The first game involved Maria Sharapova. Then after that game all the games were live on BBC TV. Sue Barker announced that the Paralympians were in the crowd. Unfortunately, when we were highlighted my friend Paul Mac had gone to the toilet and his Mum was wondering where he was. We saw the first half of a game involving Rafa Nadal and were then taken for afternoon tea, Pimms, and strawberries and cream. Following "refreshments" we went back to No. 1 Court and saw Andy Murray's first-ever game there. We eventually left after about twelve hours of a very special day.

After Athens we were invited to go to meet Tony Blair at Downing Street. I declined the invitation, as he was not my favourite person. About a year later I took part in the Paralympic World Cup in Manchester. All the sports met up for a games dinner at Manchester City's ground. I won gold, and Cherie Blair presented the medal. It caused a lot of laughter among the coaches.

I was in Wales trying to qualify for the Commonwealth Games, which I never managed. Curtis's world record had come back to haunt me. The Commonwealth Games didn't have many events for people with disabilities either. Paul Wilson was with me, and he had a new mobile phone. When we were sitting having a cup of coffee, he was speaking to someone on it and then handed it to me, but I managed to drop it straight into his coffee. It was nearly the end of a beautiful friendship. People tease me about being mean. In Wales we had to buy our own meals, and Paul W. and I ate together. Paul asked where I fancied eating, and we ended up in Sainsbury's Café. He can drive, so we were able to go to cheaper places. Paul Mac couldn't drive and always had to go to restaurants within walking distance.

Paul McInneny got a new job and was not free to travel with me to competitions. I found a new carer, Paul Wilson. I found him at the gym in Stirling. He was doing a master's degree and was working in the gym to earn some money. I was looking for a carer to travel with me. My coach's wife asked if he was interested, and that's how it all started. In 2005 there was a competition in the Czech Republic. Britain sent only two swimmers, Kenny Cairns and me, and that was Paul Wilson's first overseas trip with me. In 2005 our local MSP, Bristow Muldoon, again invited Mum, Dad, and I to see round the Scottish Parliament. We were able to hear first minister's questions, and from there went into the members' dining room for lunch. However, work goes on, and from there it was immediately back to Stirling for training.

My major competition in 2005, the Cerebral Palsy World Games, was in Connecticut. We flew from Glasgow to Reykjavik. We had four hours' wait and went for a swim in the Blue Lagoon. The swim was warm, but I didn't like the feel of the volcanic ground under my feet. Back at the airport there was a mix-up over boarding passes, and I very nearly didn't get back on the plane. Some of the team got them, and some of us didn't. The person in charge of our group was sweating because we had to wait for over an hour to have the problem sorted and he imagined half the team getting there and half being left behind. We never did find out what the problem had been. Scotland had a team in Connecticut, through Scottish Disability Sport. I was eaten alive by mosquitos, and in the opening ceremony was wearing a kilt! I hated the pool there. It was metal and had a rough surface and was in a university complex. After the competition we went training in a 50-metre pool before the lane ropes were put in. I have one dominant arm and cannot see where I'm heading, so I find it difficult to swim in a straight line when I'm doing backstroke. I ended up swimming diagonally across the pool to everyone's amusement.

Later Paul Mac and I went for a walk, and my mobile rang. It was Mum phoning me to say London had won the bid for the 2012 Olympics, at that time seven years away. I said I would never swim there. I thought I'd be retired by then. The very next day we heard about the bombings in London. One day we were happy and the next so sad. I won gold medals in Connecticut, but at that time it was to be the last CP Championships, all to do with lack of finance really. The games coincided with Fourth of July celebrations, and we witnessed some spectacular fireworks displays.

In 2006 there was a reception in Stirling Castle for sports people. Dad had to push me all the way to the top over cobbled streets. A big limousine passed us, and when the door opened it was Jack McConnell, first minister, who came across to say "Hello, Jim" and shake my hand. How we could have done with a lift, but I suppose security wouldn't allow it.

Later that year there were IPC World Championships in Durban, South Africa. After a long flight we went to a pool for a loosening swim. The pool had no changing rooms, and we had to get ready in the gardens. I could hear crickets and was sure that creepy-crawlies were going to crawl over my feet. That event was the first time I came across my Russian rival, Dmitrii Kokarev, who would go on to beat me, although I did win a gold in 50-metre freestyle and three other silver medals there. What a blow to my system after the highs of Athens. This Russian boy was young enough to be my son, and he beat me fair and square.

The country was very beautiful, but I hated the poverty. I saw a woman feeding her baby on the pavement because that's where she lived. It was just before Christmas when I came home to find everyone spending and spending and spending some more. I had left my towels behind so the maid could take them home, and I left some T-shirts for her children. It was very dangerous in Durban, and we were all advised not to go out after dark.

South Africa was where I asked my friend Graham to bleach my hair white-blonde, without my parents knowing! Paul Noble got a text from one of the girls saying "Jim's died." He thought I was deceased before realising I had changed my hair colour. On the morning of coming home it had turned blue because of the chlorine in the water. Graham was packing his bag and trying to fix my hair at the same time. He covered my hair in tomato sauce and, believe it or not, it turned blonde again. Blue was a step too far.

Every year at the Scottish National Championships in Glasgow, I was allowed to swim in the 100-metre backstroke. Scottish

Swimming made it an open event. In 2007 before I got in the water, other people with higher classifications said I wouldn't get a medal. I said, "No, I'm going to break the world record." As it happened, I did. The "old man" of the pool was the only one, including able-bodied swimmers, to get a new world record at that event. I felt like thumbing my nose at them and saying, "I told you so!"

In 2007, a year before Beijing, I went to a training camp in Macau for two weeks, an eight-hour flight landing at Hong Kong. We then had to get on a ferry to Macau, and I was nearly seasick. I was very glad to get off that boat. Macau had been used as a location for Bond movies with Roger Moore, in *The Man with the Golden Gun*, and Daniel Craig, in *Skyfall*, so we followed fine company. Our hotel in Macau was five-star and right on the beach, and we had two weeks there! We trained in a brand-new 50-metre indoor pool, although we had to be bussed to the pool and back twice a day. The British Paralympic Association ran the camp, but the British Olympic Association was also there. I saw Mo Farah there on his way to the World Cup Athletics in Osaka, Japan. During our camp all the coaches swapped round lanes so that they could get to know all the swimmers and their abilities and not just their own groups.

There was some spare time on the middle weekend, and we went into town. Paul Wilson and I went into a massive hotel with water features like a mini-Venice. It was like Las Vegas, full of slot machines, and I couldn't get over the fact it was full of little old ladies at the machines. You're not allowed to gamble in Hong Kong, so the ladies catch the ferry to Macau and gamble all day. We also had a chance to see a bit of Hong Kong. We went to a street market, and what went through my mind was *Blue Peter*. It felt like one of their summer expeditions, and very foreign. It was humid and smelly, and all sorts of goods were draped around the stalls. There were carpets, fabrics, food stuffs, bootleg CDs, DVDs, and watches, but absolutely nowhere to get a decent cup of coffee. We ended up in a back-alley cafe.

We went back to the Gold Coast in 2008 for three weeks, but this time we stayed in apartments and did our own cooking. We arrived at about 6 a.m. and had breakfast before being taken to our accommodation: a penthouse suite. We were all disappointed when two days later they moved us into a normal flat. It turned out that someone had rented out the penthouse for a two-week holiday. We had to go shopping for all our necessities, from washing up liquid to toilet rolls, and ended up with three full trollies in a huge supermarket. Paul Wilson, Andrew Lindsay, and Graham Edmonds shared the buying. Then Paul and Graham did the cooking, and Andrew did the washing-up. Graham had even bought watermelons and all sorts to make smoothies. After we trained at night we had to prepare our meals. Graham's smoothies kept us going until the meal was ready. I had developed a cold, which I managed to pass on to Graham, who was not best pleased. We had a day and a half off, but Graham had to train on the Saturday to make up for lost time. Paul and Graham had been students and had learned to cook, but some of the younger ones struggled. Mum had put two peenies (aprons) in my case for the boys. Graham wore his, but Paul threw it back at me.

Paul and Graham got fed up with me watching the Australian Open tennis championships, but I *did* do my training in one of the three pools (two 50 metres and one 25 metres) by the beach. My coach at that camp was Eddie McCluskey, and we had a great time. Before Beijing everyone was swimming using all-in-one body suits and breaking records all over the place. People thought they were brilliant. I tried one but found it made me float upright, and I couldn't swim in it at all. I qualified in May for Beijing at the Olympic and Paralympic trials in Sheffield.

Before leaving for Beijing there was a launch dinner in Birmingham at the National Indoor Arena. We were issued our kit for Beijing on Saturday morning in a local centre. Paul W. pushed me over to it, and I was fascinated by all the canals in Birmingham. There were lots of stalls at the centre advising on general health and the possibility of smog and poor air quality in Beijing, with particular warnings to those with asthma. When we got to Beijing there were no problems, but it's as well to be prepared. It seems that Chinese authorities had stopped some of the industries' activities to allow the air to clear. We were also given the chance to vote for the Team GB flag-bearer for the opening ceremony of the Games. Danny Crates, a one-armed runner, won the vote.

Two weeks before I was due to leave for Beijing, I developed phlebitis. I went to Fiona, my physio, complaining of a sore leg. She immediately phoned Dr Brian Walker at the Scottish Institute of Sport, but it was closed because they were watching the opening of the Olympics. Fiona managed to get him on his mobile, and we had to go to the institute, where he opened up the office to give me a prescription for antibiotics, giving me strict instructions to keep my feet up like Lord Muck. We raced down to the chemist in Bridge of Allan just as they were closing, and because of all their efforts, I was off training for only four days.

Beijing 2008

On our way to Beijing we stopped at a holding camp back in Macau. The night we arrived was the night of the closing ceremony of the Olympics. Instead of unpacking, we all raced to the huge television in the team room of our hotel to watch the festivities. It was all very colourful as the Chinese were winding down, but when London, as next host city, did their presentation, it all seemed very disappointing. There was a big red bus, a bus queue with black umbrellas, and David Beckham kicking a football. I thought, *Is that it?* for London's contribution. It wasn't a patch on the Chinese presentation at the Athens handover.

The Paralympic holding camp was run by a Scot, Liz Mendel, so we felt quite at home. We were there for nine days before flying on to Beijing.

I didn't go to the Paralympic opening ceremony at Beijing because I was swimming the next day. British Swimming has a rule that if you are in competition within forty-eight hours of the opening, you do not attend. It can be hot tiring and a very late finish. I stayed behind with some other competitors and let Paul Wilson go because it was his first games.

The games site was flat and easy to get about. The food hall was an enormous tent, and all types of food were available twenty-four hours a day. In the village, teams tend to keep themselves to themselves, and it feels just like being in Britain. In fact, to let us know what block of flats we were in, a red telephone box had been put outside. I couldn't get over the beautiful gardens in the games village, full of colourful flowers and water features. You could have been in Princes Street Gardens, as it didn't feel like Beijing. Only on the way to the pool did it begin to feel like China, with high-rise buildings and flashing neon advertising everywhere. The main games venues were all built close together, so huge crowds collected centrally and it was very busy.

We hung Union Jacks outside our apartment. We were drinking so much water that Matt Warwood, one of the swimmers, made a giant man out of empty water bottles. It broke up in the wind one day though, and that was the end of it. One of my teammates, Graham, knew that I wanted to dye my hair, but I hesitated about actually doing it this time. He dared me and said if I didn't do it, he was going to put me in an ice bath. I'm afraid I chickened out and had to suffer the agony of that ice bath.

We didn't have much free time and didn't see much of the contrasts of China. The National Aquatics Centre at the Beijing games was the famous Water Cube, now just a shopping centre. The warm-up pool was indoors, but you had to use huge ramps to get to it. Paul had been out before and had discovered that between the pool and the stadium, jets of water spouted up when you least expected it. One day Paul and I went for a walk outside, with him pushing my chair through the area, knowing what was likely to happen. I, in my ignorance, ended up absolutely soaked, much to Paul's amusement.

I won two silver medals and two bronzes in China. The medals were beautifully presented in a red lacquer-type box inside a silk padded box. I had to leave two of my boxes behind because I couldn't get them in my luggage, although I did keep the medals! In Athens medallists were given laurel wreaths, but in Beijing we received Chinese scrolls, in green silk boxes, recording our placings in English and Chinese. After my first race, 50-metre freestyle, we were heading for the changing rooms past the diving pool. I met Clare Balding, who was working for BBC. Again it was "Hello, Jim the Swim. How are you?" And moving on, I bumped into Marc Wood from Radio 5 Live. Once we had changed we had to attend a press conference, the first in my life. That was quite scary, sitting at a table on a platform with the other medal winners. I felt like an F1 driver at the end of a Grand Prix.

In my last race I beat my personal best, a world record, in 50-metre backstroke. The night before the race one of my friends had wound me up to think I could break my own record, which I did. Unfortunately, a Russian beat me to gold, taking my record despite my best efforts. I had competed against Dmitrii two years previously in South Africa at the World Championships, and he beat me there as well. That was the start of me losing my world number-one status. Incidentally, in Beijing I used my own goggles, specially made by Tony McGrail, using prescription lenses. Tony was both optician and swimming coach. We had met at the British Championships one year, and he asked me why I swam without goggles. I told him I couldn't see wearing goggles, so he made them for me. They made quite a difference because the roof lines and flags became much clearer. It's sometimes difficult to work out where you are when you're swimming on your back. The flags are hung over the pool to let you know that there are five metres to go to the end of the pool. My coaches spent hours shouting at me to count the strokes needed to cover those five metres, but I got so involved in the races, I quite often forgot to count. I bumped my arms, my elbows, and my head but still didn't learn to count. I could have saved points of a second off my times if I had got it right. My mother shared my coaches' frustration and tore her hair out watching me crash-land. Over the years she used to rage at me for looking round during races to check where the other competitors were. Mum and Dad always gave me a "good luck" card when I was away competing, saying, "Don't stop for a coffee break in the middle of the race!"

I did go to the closing ceremony when the IPC flag was handed on to London for safe keeping till the next games. At a closing, the current host city puts on a display by way of farewell and the next city puts on a display of invitation to their games. I was embarrassed by London's presentation that night too. It seemed unprepared and disorganised: the same red bus but with Ade Adepitan, the Paralympic basketball player, instead of David Beckham. However, after the closing the British London 2012 team and 2008 competitors went to a hotel for a party with London mayor Boris Johnson, Lord Seb Coe, and MP Tessa Jowell. It was a great night with great speeches and developed into a disco. Boris Johnston came in with the IPC flag and said, "The Paralympics are coming home." He was on good form that night. I had goosebumps but worried because I didn't think I would be able to compete in London. The pressure to succeed in London started at that point. The younger competitors were excited, but the older hands understood the great expectations of a home crowd! I was already an "old man" of forty-six, but I knew I would be at least in the crowd cheering the team on.

We had two days off after the games and went sightseeing. Paul Wilson had gone out with Eddie the night before. He was a bit under the weather the first morning when we were bussed out to the Great Wall of China. The wall is out in the mountains and is very steep in places, and the pathway is cobbled. Paul did not find it easy pushing me. From the wall you could see the smog in the valleys, although the city was clear. Lots of the Chinese people wanted their photographs taken with me because I was in my games kit. The next day Paul and I went to Tiananmen Square. What a job we had there. A taxi dropped us off but we had to go up and down underpasses because of the number of people and the eight lanes of traffic. The square is vast, and there was nothing there except a market, where Paul bought a wall hanging and people were milling about the stalls.

In Beijing I had said to Graham that I wouldn't go to the London celebration parade because I hadn't won a gold this time, but he said all medal winners were going. When I got home there was indeed an invitation waiting for me. This time Mum and Dad and I stayed at the Cumberland Hotel. The parade was to start from the Mansion House, and we had to be there by 8 a.m. Breakfast was served in the Mansion House before we were loaded on lorries and paraded round the city. Before then I had never been in the Mansion House, the official home and office of the Lord Mayor of the City of London. It is a beautiful building with wonderful paintings in long corridors.

Graham was staying in the same hotel as us, so we set off for the Mansion House together, leaving Mum and Dad to go back to bed. It was a great day. We did a typical tourist tour of London on the lorries, and at one place a man from a coffee shop ran out and served us all coffee. We ended up at Trafalgar Square, where Mum and Dad were waiting. The Paralympians went to a hotel for coffee and biscuits, after which Mum, Dad, and I went back to the Cumberland to discover that the Olympians were all having a proper lunch before going on to Buckingham Palace. The hotel staff invited us to gatecrash the lunch by the hotel staff, and we did. It would be rude to refuse! We felt happier when we discovered other Paralympians had also gatecrashed. I met Graham a week later and told him we about the lunch. He was a bit put out because he had only had a biscuit with the Paralympians. To round off our day we went to see *Joseph and the Amazing Technicolor Dreamcoat* again, at that time starring Lee Mead, who had won BBC's "Any Dream Will Do" casting competition.

It would be another month before it was the Paralympians' turn to go to the palace. This time I was with Paul Wilson. We walked from our hotel. I hadn't won any golds this time, so I wasn't taken aside, but my friend Graham Edmonds came out from that special room. He said, "Oh, you're here. They didn't want to see you this time." We had a laugh because his gold came in the relay and it took three others to get it for him.

There was a parade of champions at the British Short Course Championships at Ponds Forge, Sheffield, in November and a Scottish Parliament reception at the National Museum of Scotland. We also had a return visit to Murrayfield at the invitation of the Scottish Rugby Union to see Scotland play South Africa. I took my friend Lindsay Williamson, who was thrilled to bits, especially as we met Princess Anne. Lindsay pushed me round the track in a parade of Scottish Olympians and Paralympians before the match. Paul Wilson and I attended a Prime Minister's reception in the Natural History Museum, London, the host this time being Gordon Brown, although I never saw him. When you are in a wheelchair in a crowd with others standing round, it's quite difficult to see anything. I felt closed in and saw nothing but peoples' midriffs, not always a pleasant sight. We had travelled down in the morning, and after the reception we had quite a celebration in a pub before travelling back the next day.

In December we were swimming at the Welsh Open Championships. On the Sunday some of us went to Liverpool Quays for the BBC Sports Personality of the Year recording. It was a bit of a rush because we only had half an hour to book into our hotel, change, and get to the Quays. This was the first time the event had been held outside London, and it was in a huge arena. The audience was not just invited sportsmen and women as in previous years. Members of the public had also been invited. We wheelchair users were sitting in the front row at floor level, but Paul had to sit further back in the audience. Chris Hoy won it that year. He spotted me in the corridor at the end of the night and told his friends to go on because he wanted to chat with me. Paul thinks we look alike and calls me Chris's big brother! After the recording there was a party where the wine was flowing freely, and we had eaten nothing but nibbles all day. We ended up a little tiddly and went back to our hotel at about 2 a.m. I went to bed and fell sound asleep. Sometime during the night Paul got up to go to the toilet but mistook the door and ended up in the corridor rather than the bathroom. He banged and banged on the door to get in, but I was so sound asleep I never heard him. He had to go down to reception in his boxer shorts to get the pass key. In the morning we had to wait for Paul to sober up before he could drive us home.

Following Beijing I got a new coach, Kerry Wood, who was to make me ready for European Championships in 2009, to be held in Iceland. We had to qualify for those championships at a Disability Sport England Championships in Sheffield in April 2009. Needless to say, it was cold in Iceland in autumn. The warm-up and warm-down pools were outside, and when we competitors were in these pools, our coaches and carers were wrapped up in big coats and hats. I call it "cruelty to competitors". One day it was so cold after training that Paul put us in the spa hot tub to warm up again. I had a real job to get back out of it. Graham Edmonds had to help me out because he was still in trunks and Paul Wilson was fully dressed and didn't fancy getting wet. I beat my Russian rival in that competition, winning gold, two silvers, and a bronze. Everyone was flabbergasted that I had finally beaten Dmitrii. The indoor competition pool was like the old Leeds pool with an off-set roof, and I think the Russian didn't know where he was. That's how I beat him. One of the medals was awarded in a relay. These were 20-point relays, meaning that the classifications of the team members should add up to no more than 20. As my classification is 2, it meant that the remaining points could be divided among more able teammates. It evens out across the teams very well.

Iceland was where I had an argument with the head coach. The competition had finished on Saturday evening, but he wanted us all to swim again on Sunday morning. I told him I didn't want to swim on the Sabbath. He pushed me in anyway, so I didn't get away with it. On the last night Paul and I bought a pizza. It cost £20, and Paul nearly had a heart attack. We visited the Blue Lagoon, but I didn't go in this time, as I had been in the lagoon on the stopover in 1995 on the way to the States. I went instead for a coffee with Derek Martin, team doctor. Our flight was like a circular tour. We went direct to Reykjavik but returned via Manchester and back to Edinburgh.

When I got home on Sunday after the qualifying event championships in Sheffield, Mum and Dad said, "What a weekend we've had." On the Saturday the postman had come with a letter from the prime minister saying I had been nominated for an Officer of the Order of the British Empire (OBE) in the Queen's birthday honours list. Mum read the letter out to me, and I was speechless. "What are you on about? I already have an MBE. People like us don't get OBEs." They had had all this exciting news and couldn't tell anyone. We had to wait till it was officially announced. On that Saturday morning we went to the weekly coffee morning at the church, and people broke into applause, all very embarrassing, compounded by the minister announcing it again in church on Sunday. I was surprised that among all the cards and letters that came in, there was one from my former OT from school, a delightful thought.

My investiture was at Buckingham Palace again, and this time we took my cousin Anne. My mother was going to wear a fascinator, but I was determined she should wear a hat. I won, even though she'd had to adapt it to match the colour of her outfit. We had great fun transporting the hat in its box all the way to London. Mind you Mum had transferred the hat from its original huge box into a smaller British Home Stores one, covering up the logo with a fashion picture cut out of a glossy magazine. Mum, Dad, and Anne were allocated special seats in the ballroom, and I was pushed by one of the Palace officials. This time Dad could watch this time, and I wasn't quite as nervous, as I vaguely remembered the procedure. We heard Princess Anne arriving by helicopter to do the investitures that day. Mum said, "Imagine the Princess Royal flying in just to give you your OBE." As she was pinning the OBE to my kilt jacket, Princess Anne asked me whether I would be at London 2012. I told her that if I wasn't swimming, I would be in the crowd cheering everyone on. Strangely, at the investiture I met a lady also receiving an MBE who knew our minister and her husband. It's really a small world. When we came out of the Palace there were lots of schoolchildren gathering to watch the Changing of the Guard. I ended up having many photos taken because I was wearing my kilt. The guards appeared to be second choice.

After the investiture, we had lunch in Gary Rhodes's restaurant, and at night we went to see *Calendar Girls* at the theatre. My other claim to fame over that was that my photo appeared in the *Daily Record* when the honours list was made public! After Athens and my four golds and two world records, the MBE was the icing on the cake, but my OBE was the cherry on top. When we came back from London the huge tsunami disaster in the Far East had happened. To raise money, Broxburn Parish Church held a coffee afternoon and played the DVD of my investiture as part of the fundraising effort.

In 2010 before I went to Holland for a World Championships, the other athletes and I had a camp in Majorca. I managed to break my bed there. It collapsed as I fell onto it. The pool was so close, we could walk from the hotel. The evenings were warm, and Paul Wilson and I would go out for walks. It was on this trip that Paul got me hooked on iced coffee. Derek Martin has a tendency to go walk-about at times too, probably to get a breather from us all. He disappeared in Majorca and went into an ironmonger's and came back with a piece of plastic tubing. He thought I was not sucking in enough of my asthma treatment from my inhalers and rigged up the piping to my inhalers so that I could draw in more of the powder into my airways. I have to admit that it worked well. He can wander off any time he likes!

In Eindhoven, Holland, at the World Championships, all the teams stayed in the same hotel. We sat around in a large old-fashioned library room with leather armchairs, all very Victorian. I won three silver medals, beaten again by my Russian rival. That was the last competition where I swam 200 metres – a long way for an old man like me.

There was a lovely walk through a park from the hotel to the pool. One day after the morning heats Paul and Rob came up with the great idea that it would be quicker walking back to the hotel, as there was no shuttle bus waiting. They took what they thought was a shortcut but found a locked gate we just couldn't open. By this time we were getting desperate for the toilet. We had to go back the way we had come, and it ended up with Paul and Rob running, pushing Fran Williams and me in our chairs to finally get back to the hotel, to the relief of all. After the swimming we went to watch an open-water event a few miles away, not something I ever fancied trying!

That year I didn't have qualifying times to keep my lottery funding, so I took Paul Mac with me to a meet in Wales, my last chance. I liked having Paul with me in stressful situations. He even shaved me down on the Friday to maximise my chances. As I walked into the pool with Paul, our head coach, Lars, said, "Anderson means business! He's brought his lucky sidekick." I was very nervous, but one of the swimmers, Nyree, told me to stop moaning and get in the water and swim. I had to wait till the last race of the event before I managed the necessary time to continue in training and competition.

In January 2011 we had training camps, and at Stirling we had a fire drill. We were all evacuated outside in our pyjamas. Luckily, there were only two swimmers and two staff at that camp. It was snowing overnight, and in the morning at 6 a.m. we all got into cars to go down to the pool. Rob opened the back window of his car and said, "Right, Jim, you push the snow off the window." In my innocence I tried. Instead of it falling outwards, it came inwards, and I was wet and cold before we even got close to the water. At another training camp, this time at Dunblane Hydro, there was a real fire, and we were not allowed back into our rooms. We were all evacuated to another hotel in Stirling, about halfway up the castle hill. Jill, our coach, went off to buy us toothbrushes and basic toiletries. She must have told some good sob stories because the supermarket supplied them all free. Paul McInneny and I went shopping, and when we were coming back up the hill, he made me get out of my wheelchair and push him for a change.

For the second training week in January the Stirling four flew down to Manchester. It was blowing a gale, and it was the worst flight I have ever been on. It was extremely turbulent, and I was nearly sick. I was very frightened, but Paul Wilson burst out laughing. Rob Aubry, one of the coaches, was sitting in the row in front of me with his hands over his neck in case I was going to be sick over him. We landed safely and went to our hotel, but the others played a trick on me. They put me in a room that had a bell outside the door and told me that when I went into my room I should get onto my bed quickly because a bell would go off. When I was lying on my bed I was supposed to give a thumbs-up to a box high up in the corner of the room, and the bell would stop. Little did I know that Rob was outside the door with his finger on the bell! It took me two days to work it out. Who was dafter though, me or them, because they kept ringing that bell for two days?

In April 2011, at the time of Prince William and Kate Middleton's wedding, there were German Open Championships in Berlin. I was disappointed to miss all the excitement at home in Britain. However, I was entered in three races in Berlin. Afterwards we were sitting in the cafe enjoying a well-earned coffee and discovered that German television was showing the royal wedding, so I saw it after all. All the girls in the team agreed that Kate's dress was very beautiful.

Later in the year we were back in Berlin. We stayed in a huge hotel, and my room was enormous, with a king-size bed. The room could have taken my living room and kitchen at home with space to spare. It was one of the few events where all the competitors were accommodated in one hotel. The pool was in an old wartime underground bunker, but the roof looked just like a piece of derelict land. We were able to walk out of the hotel and across to a lift which took us down to the pool. I won four silver medals, but more surprising at this stage of my swimming career, I came up with a personal best and a new British record in 100-metre freestyle. Paul Wilson asked, "Where did that come from?" But I was as amazed and as excited as he was.

After that meet in Germany the British swim team went on a secret trip to the new Olympic pool in London in October 2011. Nobody knew we were there. We had travelled down to London the night before and stayed in a Hilton. What an epic journey! In the space of thirty-six hours, I was in a car, a plane, a bus, a train, a ferry, and a tube train. Mum and Dad took me to Edinburgh Airport by car. All the medallists had been given a pass for the executive lounge, and we were given a free lunch. Paul McInneny and I flew to Heathrow and went by train to Paddington Station. Paul was worried on the train that we were going the wrong way, but it was okay. A taxi was next to the Hilton in Docklands. The hotel appeared to be built in three parts, with water in between. There were bridges inside the hotel over Thames water and an old dry dock, a very original feature, leading to the public rooms and bedrooms. For our evening meal we got a ferry across the river. In the morning we had a buffet-style breakfast before getting the ferry to catch up with the rest of the team. We walked to Docklands Light Railway and on to Stratford, where we met up outside the station. We were told to get some lunch at the kiosk and after that we had to be issued with passes. I had difficulty getting my pass because I was supposed to hold my hand flat on a machine that would read my fingerprints. Because of my cerebral palsy, I couldn't hold my hand steady for long enough. I eventually got my pass, and we were bussed to the pool, at that stage still a building site.

It was the first time ever I've been to a swimming event in Britain and had to go through airport-type security to get in. We changed in a corridor because the changing rooms were not ready. Mind you, even for the Paralympics there were no lockers in place. We had to put our kit in bags and take it with us to poolside. We had a swim in the main competition pool and then had a tour of the building. It was very exciting, and the building looked bigger than at other games. The seats seemed to go up to the sky. It all felt very creepy because there was nobody there and the place was silent. We all felt we had to whisper. It was good to see the new pool, especially as I didn't know if I would be on the team for London 2012. Then it was tube train, train, flight, and car to get back home, and all in thirty-six hours. I found the tube quite scary because we managed to hit it in the rush hour. It was absolutely packed, and I felt very vulnerable.

Paul W. and I went to the Welsh Open Championships in December 2011 and were chatting in the car on the way down. I wondered if I should carry on to try for the London games. Paul told me not to be stupid, as I had come up with a personal best only three months earlier.

In March 2012 we had Olympic and Paralympic qualifying meets. Mum, Dad, Paul Mac, and I stayed in an apartment near the pool in London. We went down by train on the Saturday and took a taxi to the flats. Because nothing was provided, we had to go and get shopping. A group from Scottish Swimming was staying in the same block and advised us where to find a supermarket. It was like being back on the Gold Coast again. We had to buy everything from table salt to toilet rolls. Coming back, my chair was loaded with all the heavy stuff, and everyone else carried at least one bag of groceries.

When the heats and races came along, I had never been so nervous poolside. If I qualified, all my family would be able to come and see me in a "home" game. The pressure started to build. I narrowly missed the qualifying time because I had hit a lane rope. There were no heats or finals, just a straight swim against the clock, and hitting that rope was enough to spoil my chances. I was gutted to miss out. By this time, for the first time in my entire swimming career, I had a sports psychologist, Mischa Botting. Mischa was at that meet working with able-bodied swimmers, but Paul W. spoke to him and said, "Jim needs to talk to you. He's low because he hasn't made the team." It was very helpful having Mischa there. He helped me get through that week.

At the end of the week, we were taken on a bus tour of the Olympic park and then British Gas took the swim team on a boat trip on the Thames. It was a queer day. Some people were high because they had got their time, while the rest of us were very nervous since we knew we only had one more chance. I made life at home a hell for my parents, and I don't know how they put up with me.

My last chance came a month later in Sheffield. I missed the time again, but only by one one-thousandth of a second. I came back from Sheffield on the Monday and didn't sleep for two days until the team was announced at mid-day on Wednesday. I had been so close to qualifying that I was allowed on the team and was on to my sixth Paralympics. There was a long list of potential competitors at a training camp in Manchester a year before London, and we all had to be measured for our kits. When my selection letter arrived with all my measurements enclosed, my mother noticed that they were all wrong. She had to remeasure me and submit the correct ones; otherwise I wouldn't have been able to get into my London uniform.

London 2012

During the month after getting our selection letters, we had lots of meetings, and Mum had a lot of form-filling and paperwork to deal with concerning entries for the Paralympics. I had meetings with Kerry, my coach, to plan my training programme for the twelve weeks leading up to the games so that I could be in peak condition. Kerry suggested that I should stop swimming in the short Broxburn pool and go five days a week to Stirling to concentrate on work in the 50-metre pool. British Swimming was worried that I only swam at night and was not an early-morning person. Most heats are swum in the mornings. I ended up being in the water in Stirling at 9 a.m. on Monday mornings, which meant that Mum and Dad had to be up early to take me through. On Monday mornings I swam; Tuesday I swam later in the day; Wednesday I had afternoon sessions doing weight training and gym work before swimming again; Thursday was physio before more work in the water; and Friday was a repeat of Wednesday, with weights and a swim. By the weekend I felt like a zombie, and that programme continued for nearly all those twelve weeks.

Before I went to the London Games, it seemed the training was getting harder and harder. It was becoming difficult to get motivated. I felt like my commitment was going, but I knew I should persevere because it was a home games. Everywhere I went all the papers and TV channels were going on about London, London, London. One day I was excited, the next apprehensive – up and down like a yo-yo about London. In my head I was counting down how many more training days before I could give up. I was desperate to go to London but desperate to stop as well. I was getting more and more tired, and age was against me. I was taking longer to recover after each session. In the build-up, I began to feel excited, although I knew by that time that this would be my Paralympics swansong. International competition is really a younger person's game, and I was finding it more and more of a struggle to do the necessary slog. Mum and Dad were also finding the transport to training a bit of a trial after all these years.

Olympic fever was hitting the rest of Scotland too! Every year our church holds an Easter mission, really a children's holiday club. The programme in 2012 was, naturally, based on an Olympic theme, and each group of youngsters was given the name of one of the previous Olympic venues. As so many of the children know me, I was asked to bring medals from games I had already attended. They got to put the medals round their necks like a proper presentation, and it helped to make the games more real for them. I was also invited to go along to local primary schools, both in Broxburn and Comely Park in Falkirk, where my cousin's granddaughter Skye-Rose was a pupil. She had a great time bragging to her classmates about her "Uncle Jim" and telling them about my exploits. I took videos of the Athens games and, again, some medals. The children were so excited to see in real life what they had only seen on television. It is important to encourage young folk to be all they can be and to let them see what people with disabilities can achieve. Although it was fun to do, it was another task added to the intense five-day training regime.

There was a short break in that routine in May when the GB Paralympic swim team had a get-together at a two-week training camp in Majorca. It was to be no holiday, and Paul W. said it would be the hardest bit of the twelve-week cycle, a fitness camp. It certainly was hard work. I was swimming twice a day and still had to do the weight training and gym work. The heat also added to the general feeling of healthy fatigue. During the middle weekend of the camp, British Swimming raised the subject of swimwear for the team. They were keen for the male swimmers to wear skins, sort of knee-length shorts. Paul W. and Rob decided they could never get me into these skins, but Graham said, "Let's try a pair." After lots of laughter, Rob had the idea of putting bin liners over my feet and legs, pulling the skins over the top, and then pulling the bags off again. It worked, and that performance continued until the end of my swimming career. In Majorca as well as all the physical work, we had training in dealing with the media. As the home team at a home games, it seemed we were likely to be in the spotlight. Despite our busy schedules, Paul and I still managed to have our usual outings for ice cream and coffee. But soon it was back to the slog of five days a week at Stirling.

In June the Olympic torch made its way round Britain in preparation for London, and Broxburn was one of the places it passed through before going on to Edinburgh. The day was beautifully sunny and became a real carnival. The town was packed. Our church and its halls became a central point for refreshments and exhibitions, and a base for the various school choirs, bands, and samba drummers. As part of the exhibitions, I had been asked to provide a display of some of my medals, trophies, and other awards. Mum and Dad sat on guard and explained to everyone who was interested what all the awards were. I was asked to be part of the parade, and my friend Graham Taylor was to push my chair. No rest for the wicked though, as I still had to complete my training programme in Broxburn pool that morning before the fun started.

I leant Graham one of my GB International jackets, so he really looked the part. We had to line up at the local primary school and were accompanied by the West Lothian School's pipe band, the Broxburn brass band, and majorettes. We were towards the front of the parade and moved off about half a mile, with everyone behind us. When we reached the end of the parade route, we dispersed and rushed back to see the torch itself, which was very near the back of the procession. The trouble was that we were going against all the traffic. We got back to the church hall, and the local children wanted photos of me with some of my medals. I wanted to see the torch, but a man in the crowd wouldn't let me through. One of the church ladies pointed out that I was in a wheelchair and he could see over me. She also pointed out to him that I would be going to the London games as a competitor. Suddenly I was at the front, and when I saw the torch, I had a shiver down my back! It was all becoming very real. It was definitely party time in Broxburn.

It took us three hours, instead of the usual ten minutes, to get home because of the crowds. Olympic mania was definitely building. I had the luxury of a "local" event on the last weekend of June when the Scottish National Championships were held in the Royal Commonwealth Pool in Edinburgh. It had been closed for refurbishment for a long time, and the event was almost a grand reopening. I was reasonably happy with my swims as the weeks passed.

One day Mum, Dad, and I were sitting in the living room about midday watching television when a courier's delivery van arrived. Dad's comment was "What are we getting now?" It turned out to be two big boxes full of sporting kit designed by Stella McCartney. There were training shoes, flip-flops, polo shirts, hoodies, tracksuits, four different hats (baseball caps and beanie hats), sunglasses, backpacks, and a towel. Everything was blue and bright red. The swimming gear came later. All my gear, including socks, had to be labelled with my name, and Mum had a lot of work to do for me. Laundry is done for us at the games, and at least we would be sure of getting our own kits back. The only games where the laundry service nearly didn't happen was Sydney, but the ladies there said they were going to do it for us despite what the authorities said, as they'd done it for the able-bodied competitors.

One Saturday in July I had to get my parents up to get me into Edinburgh to catch the 7 a.m. train to Kings Cross for the official Paralympics team launch. All the Scottish swimmers travelled down together, and we took taxis over the Thames to our hotel from the Houses of Parliament. We were then issued with a formal suit for posh occasions, walking-out gear, and an outfit for the closing ceremony. We had, for the opening, a white and gold outfit of white trousers, white T-shirt with gold lions on the back, a white jacket with a hood (also with a gold lion on the back), white socks with lions, and white shoes. The closing outfit was a navy cardigan, red trousers, a white T-shirt with a red-and-blue sequined lion, and blue socks with lions. Paul W. said he needed dark glasses when he was helping me to try the outfits on! A team of tailors was on duty to alter all the kit to fit and accommodate the particular needs of amputees, specific heights, and any other differences that any large group of people has. Each competitor had an allocated thirty-minute slot for final fitting. We had to gather at 2 p.m. and be suited and booted by 5.30 p.m. When I went to be fitted, my trousers were too long and I only got them back at 5.30, so it was a mad dash to be ready.

The launch was to be at a BT (British Telecom) celebration dinner at Old Billingsgate. On our way to the meal, we passed the Tower of London and were told that all the Olympic and Paralympic medals were safely under lock and key inside. At that dinner, I heard the British Paraorchestra for the first time, made up of professional musicians all with disabilities. Some of the athletes were even persuaded to parade in their newly acquired outfits. We eventually got back to our hotel at 1 a.m. and settled into our enormous room. Paul and I had a double bed each, with a huge bathroom in the middle. On the Sunday morning, we had to be up with tracksuits on at 7.30 a.m. to have a Paralympic team photo taken of competitors and support staff in Parliament Square in front of Westminster. It had to be taken early, before too many of the general public were up and about. There were two rows of wheelchairs, one up a level, and four standing rows – quite a big team.

After that the swim team had a meeting but didn't get to go home yet. We moved on to Sheffield for a weeklong competition, officially a youth gala, and me forty-nine years old at that stage! We travelled up to Sheffield by train, where Mum and Dad were already waiting. They were going to be my carers for the week, as Paul had to be back at work in Stirling. Paul phoned them from the train to let them know when we would be arriving, but Dad said they were out on the street because of yet another hotel fire, a feature in my life. When Paul came off the phone, he wound me up again by saying, "At least I've got a bed for the night. You'll be sleeping in the car park." At that gala in Sheffield the American Olympic diving team was using the diving pool, as Sheffield was their holding camp. Normally we used the diving pool for our swim-downs but had to use the leisure pool, doing circles of the pool under the flumes. It was strange knowing that this was our last competition before the London 2012 Paralympics.

We came home from Sheffield and went back to the daily grind of the trek to Stirling. I did two more step tests of 50-metre repeats, swimming against the clock to check how my times were going and to put some extra pressure on, in preparation for competition. Mum had to pack up all my kit for London. This time our holding camp was in Manchester in August, not quite as exciting as Macao or Cyprus. The Scottish contingent all left together by train from Edinburgh, and we had a great send-off from family and friends at the crack of dawn on a Sunday morning. Our accommodation in Manchester was again in a Hilton, with penthouse suites where some of the super-rich footballers lived. Paul W. took our bags up to our room but left me with a bagful of kit to swap. Half of our kit fitted, but it was a bit of a bun fight trying to swap the half that didn't. We swapped around what still didn't fit when we got to London. We had to be dressed in our games uniforms at 6.30 p.m. for a reception that had been laid on for us. For the reception, the team was taken up to a level just below the penthouses. It had a glass floor and a wonderful view out over Manchester.

On the Monday morning hard work started again in the two 50-metre pools built for the Manchester Commonwealth Games. Underneath the main pool was the main base for British Disabled Swimming. During that week, we had to have yet another team photo taken, and this time they put boards over the diving pool for us to stand on. Needless to say, the boards sagged under the strain, and everyone ended up getting their feet wet. We did our final preparations, swimming twice a day, with a lot of resting in between. Carl Payton took the last filming of my starts and turns to analyse for any last-minute tweaks. Tension in the team was building: a mixture of excitement, nervousness, and pressure. For relaxation, various activities were organised for the evenings. One night they held a fancy dress karaoke. I was dressed up in a black wig as John Travolta, and one of the girls, Kate Grey, sat on my knee to sing "You're the One That I Want" from *Grease*. After much laughter, we won! Kate is now a BBC sports presenter. I like to think I gave her a start in showbiz!

At the end of the week, I thought, *Well, this is it; we're on our way to our home games.* I was full of nervous anticipation. We were going on to London by train, and when we were in a bus waiting to be taken to the station a passing Gay Pride Carnival parade entertained us. I had never seen a Gay Pride procession before. It was all very colourful and noisy – quite an experience. A special first-class train had been laid on for us. We had a great laugh on the train when some of the more mobile swimmers went up to see the driver. They came back boasting that they had driven the train. It was a good job we didn't know about it at the time. When we got to London, buses came right onto the platform to take us to the games village. I felt like royalty.

When we arrived at the security gate of the village, there was a thunder storm and torrential rain. However, we managed to get through security very quickly, getting our passes without too much delay or fuss. It was the quickest I have ever been through the authorisation process and security checks at any Paralympics. It felt like the London Organising Committee had done its research and got it right. The London games were the best organised I have been to.

After passing through security, we were bussed round to our apartments. Each block had metal railings round it, and it was a little like going back to Edwardian London, with wheelchairs rather than horse-drawn carriages. Our flat was on the third floor. Luckily, there were lifts. The view was spectacular over London, away to Canary Wharf and the Gherkin. I went into my room and said to Paul, "There are a lot of plugs in here." It turned out that my room was to be the kitchen when the apartments became housing after the games. There were four of us in the flat, and it was great company.

The next morning, we were taken for a tour of the village and discovered there were shops, hairdressers, and post offices where you could have your own photo printed on stamps. I bought fifty with my photo on and used them later for the invitations to my fiftieth birthday party. There was a big store selling Olympic Games souvenirs of all types. One night when we got back to the flat, there was a huge bar of Cadbury's chocolate for each competitor, and each had our name printed on the wrapper, a personal gift. I called Paul through, but he said, "Don't talk about it. I don't want to know. There isn't one on my bed!" Only competitors were given one, not the staff.

The day before the official opening ceremony, each competing nation's flag was raised in the village. A theatre group performed a circus act, and Dame Tanni Grey-Thompson made a speech of welcome just for the athletes, before the dignitaries arrived for the official opening. The honour of being flag-bearer at the opening is voted for by all the athletes. Each sport nominates someone, and I was thrilled that my teammates proposed me. The ultimate honour went to Peter Norfolk, the wheelchair tennis player.

Before the opening Paul and I went for a meal at about 3 p.m. The food hall was enormous and open twenty-four hours, serving all sorts of food. We were all warned beforehand to have only one main meal a day because it was all too easy to overindulge. Next door to our block was the medical centre, and just beyond that was an open-air barbecue area, again open all day. After our meal Paul and I went back to our apartment to get into our white outfits for the opening parade. We were bussed to the arena, and because it was so wet, we were put into the volunteers' canteen to wait. It was three hours before it was our turn. We were able to watch most of the opening on a screen in the canteen. Officials came and lined us up ready for our entrance. At the opening of the games, Team GB, as the hosts, was last in the parade of nations. We came up through a tunnel under the stands and into the arena, all shouting "GB, GB, GB!" The noise of the crowd was like hitting a wall of sound. It was wet, but the crowd's enthusiasm made up for all the rain.

At the opening the emphasis was on ability and achievement of people with disabilities. People in wheelchairs were "flown" into the arena. One of them was Marc Wood, my flatmate from Barcelona. There was a disabled acrobat – in fact all sorts of people with all sorts of skills. Her Majesty the Queen performed the official opening. The fireworks at the end were fantastic, and I eventually got into my bed about 12.45 a m. I had to be up for training the next morning, and that was difficult.

I don't know what it was about competing in London; maybe I was aware that it would be my last swim in the Paralympics; maybe it was because it was a home games and there was a lot of hype since my friends and family were able to come and support me. Mum and Dad and three cousins and all their families came wearing T-shirts saying "I love Jim the Swim" on the front. Dad's had "Jim the Swim's Dad" on the back. The biggest surprise I got was meeting some of my old swimming pals, some of whom I hadn't seen since Barcelona. It was day four of the games before I was due to swim, but every day we went to the pool to support other members of the team. It also helped us get used to the volume of noise from the crowd and the light levels around the building. Even Prince William came and joined the team at poolside for some of the finals.

The aquatic centre was crowded for every heat and every final. The noise was tremendous. I had three events: 100-metre freestyle, 50-metre backstroke, and 50-metre freestyle. In the heats for the 100-metre freestyle, when the British swimmers were called out, the noise was unbelievable – a home games right enough. I came fourth in my heat and made the final, in which I was placed eighth. In that first final, the coaches noticed I was very subdued. I was simply very nervous because of the weight of expectation I had put on myself. Normally I was pumped up and trying to psyche out the other competitors, but not this time. For my second event, the 50-metre backstroke, Paul and Rob wound me up and got me high. I won my heat, beating my old rivals Dmitrii Kokarev and Curtis Lovejoy, and was placed in lane five for the final. I came fourth, the worst position of all: just outside the medals. But at least I can say I won a race in London, even if it was only a heat. The gold medallist was a sixteen-year-old Chinese boy. I was old enough to be his granddad! I felt a bit happier because I had done a reasonable time and it was good to see younger people able to take the sport forward. Everyone was satisfied with my effort despite the result.

The 50-metre freestyle was to be my last race, and everything that could go wrong in the heats did so. I hit a lane line, which literally knocked me off my stroke, and I ended up doing a couple of double-arm strokes, losing momentum. My goggles filled with water and I couldn't see what was happening. It was very bad, and I ended up in a disastrous tenth place overall. It was the first time ever I hadn't made a final, and what made it worse was it was only 50 metres, a single length with no turn to worry about. I have never felt so miserable and upset. There was a wee quiet room where people could take time out and reflect or pray or just try to focus. When Doc Martin and Paul hauled me out of the water and into my wheelchair, I went in there and bawled and shouted at God in anger. I blamed Him for my lack of success. It took a long time to get over the disappointment and feeling of failure. The only people I could talk to at the time were Doc Martin and my friend Graham Edmond. I felt so ashamed and lonely. After the race I apologised to my two cousins for bringing them down to London just to see me in such a disastrous race. All three of us were in tears, and I think Mum was hiding! It took Paul and Kerry a whole day to come and speak to me, I was so unapproachable.

Despite my feelings, there were many successes and high points for Team GB. One night we were sitting in our apartment with the door open watching the telly when there was a huge roar from the stadium. It was Jonnie Peacock winning the 100-metre sprint. The noise was so loud we heard it over the telly back in our flat.

On Saturday, the last day of swimming, Andy Mullen and I had finished our competitions and Paul, and Rob walked us back to the accommodation through the Olympic Park. The gardens were beautiful, and I couldn't get over the number of people around. It seemed like the biggest crowd I'd seen at a games. As we were moving through the crowd, we came across a Mexican mariachi band wearing large sombreros and playing guitars and trumpets. Needless to say, we had to have our photos taken with them. At the end of the event all the medallists had their photos taken, but Graham Edmond wanted photos of those of us who hadn't won anything. We had to pose with petted lips and miserable faces.

I went to the closing ceremony on Sunday evening, but Doc Martin and I really felt our ages. The bands (Coldplay, Rihanna, and Jay Z) were for the younger people, although the British Paraorchestra was excellent. I felt strange because at previous closings I was excited about where we were going next. I felt a bit numb when Ellie Simmonds was putting out the flame. I knew I wouldn't be back, and it definitely felt like the end of an era. Everyone else was singing and dancing about, whereas I just felt empty and sad, but relieved in a way. The slog was over and I could get my life back!

After all the closing celebrations we were expected to be up and ready to leave the village at 7.30 a.m. on the Monday morning. Olympians and Paralympians were to get onto floats to be taken on a celebration parade round the centre of London. We had been partying into the early hours, and during the evening Kerry and I watched the final of the US Masters tennis on a big screen in a pub. I was not alone that Monday feeling a little unwell! While we were in the Mansion House waiting for the floats, I fell asleep – one of the benefits of using a wheelchair. Paul Wilson woke me up with a can of Red Bull to get me up and going. There were more people than ever waiting for the parade. The Olympic spirit was still about in London. The route took us from the Mansion House, passing St Paul's, down Ludgate Hill, and out onto Fleet Street. People were hanging out of every office window as well as filling all the pavement space. We travelled along the Strand and passed through Trafalgar Square, where there was a big screen showing the progress of all the floats, courtesy of the BBC. Then we went through Admiralty Arch and down the Mall to Buckingham Palace. There was nowhere along the route where there was a gap in the crowds. As we went down the mall I saw a woman in the crowd with a banner saying "Jim the

Swim". As I hadn't won any medals, I didn't think anyone would be interested, but it was a woman from the Scottish Swimming office. It was a really lovely surprise.

There were twenty-one floats, and when we got off we went round to the Albert Memorial. There were so many Olympians and Paralympians that we totally surrounded the memorial. It was such a lovely day. I put all my disappointment on the back burner and tried to enjoy myself, as I knew this would be the last time. It wasn't easy. As we passed Buckingham Palace Doc Martin said, "It's a pity your Auntie Lizzie's not in." He was teasing me because I had been into the Palace so often over the years. Boris Johnson and Seb Coe made speeches in celebration of the games, and a reception hosted by David Cameron at the Queen Elizabeth Second Conference Centre followed. The whole group of athletes walked down to the reception. Thank goodness it all happened on the same day and we didn't have to go back down to London later. A meal and disco were laid on, and David Cameron made a speech. At the end of the function the Paralympians made their way back to the Olympic village, where the celebrations continued.

That was the lead-in to another hectic week. We left for home on Tuesday, flying back to Edinburgh. Kerry, at that time, had two children, and when workers were dismantling the Olympic venue, she acquired two six-foot cardboard Olympic mascots, which came back on the plane with us. I don't know how we got away with it. On the journey, Kerry advised me to take a complete two-week break away from training and swimming to think about my plans for the future. I had no medals from London, but I did have chocolate with "Jim Anderson, OBE" on it. I also brought home my commemorative event duvet and pillowcases, kindly given by the manufacturers, for both Olympians and Paralympians. It's great to think these items are all round the world now.

On Wednesday of that busy week, Mum was going frantic because on the Friday there was to be a parade and reception for Scottish Olympic and Paralympic competitors in Glasgow, and that night there was also the Scottish Swimming Awards night dinner.

Luckily, the dinner was also in Glasgow. Mum couldn't see how we could fit it all in because I had to have two outfits: my tracksuit for the parade and my formal games suit and tie for the dinner. To complicate matters, I had come back from London minus my "uniform" black shoes and had lost my Olympic tie. Next supplied the formal outfits for the games and were having a sale at the time, so we sent my cousin Betty off on an unsuccessful mission to buy another pair of black shoes. I ended up wearing shoes from the Beijing games and ended up with very sore feet.

Mum, dad, and I decided to stay in Glasgow overnight. So when Friday came, we went to our hotel to get changed. I got into my tracksuit, and Mum and Dad took me by taxi to meet Paul at Kelvin Grove where the parade was to start. Cousin Betty was there too, and after she saw us off she took Mum and Dad back to the hotel for them to get ready for the evening. Meanwhile the lorries took us through Glasgow to the City Chambers in George Square. I remember it being sunny and hot, and I couldn't get over the size of the crowds in George Square. My friend Jill Douglas was the compère and introduced us all to the people. Inevitably I was introduced as "Jim the Swim". Paul was amazed that I, as a non-medal winner, was introduced – and I was a little surprised too.

There was a reception afterwards hosted by Alex Salmond, but none of the swimmers could go, because we had to get to the awards dinner at the Glasgow Science Centre on the banks of the Clyde. We came off the stage at George Square and got onto a specially chartered double-decker bus to get to the Glasgow Science Centre, where Mum and Dad were waiting in their finery with my Paralympic suit. All the athletes had to change out of our Paralympic tracksuits and into our formal suits for the occasion. I had my wrong black shoes, but Craig Rodgie, another competitor, had two Paralympics ties and gave me one to wear at the dinner. They presented me with a picture of me at the end of one of my London races. We stayed in Glasgow overnight and travelled back on the Saturday morning.

My poor mother then had to wash and press my tracksuit for a very special parade in Edinburgh – very special because the now knighted Sir Chris Hoy was to receive the Freedom of the City of Edinburgh. All the Lothian Olympians and Paralympians were invited, and after a buffet we were taken by open-topped bus from the City Chambers, down the Mound to the assembly rooms in George Street for the freedom ceremony. For the first time in my life I was upstairs on a doubler-decker and really enjoyed the experience, even though I was huddled under an umbrella because of the pouring rain. Mum and Dad were sensibly sitting downstairs in the dry, and my cousins were in a following bus. Going down the Mound, I spotted two friends, Ross MacPherson and Kenny Turnbull, in the crowd and waved. I was in trouble though because I hadn't waved to Kenny Young, who was on the other side of the road. It was very special to see Sir Chris Hoy being honoured by the City of Edinburgh. He always took time to speak to me when we met up over the years. The Freedom is not often given. While Sir Chris got his parchment, the rest of us received mementos to add to our many memories of the occasion.

At the start of the next week, it all went flat. I had a lot to think about. I felt numb, disappointed, and angry with myself, and I just wanted to hide. I was emotionally drained. I thought, *I just can't give up my swimming career after that pig's ear of a final race. It's not good to go out on such a low.* All I could think about was that swim and that I'd let down all my family and friends. I was scared to go to church and meet people because I hadn't won any medals. I was sure people would ignore me since my homecoming hadn't been triumphal, like after previous games. We have a lunchtime service on Wednesdays, and I plucked up courage to speak to two of my friends, Graham Taylor and Sally North, about how I was feeling. They both told me not to be so hard on myself and that people like me for who I am rather than what I have done. Gradually I recovered my confidence.

After my two-week break from training and swimming, I went back to Stirling to meet Kerry and Paul Wilson, now Disability Performance Development Manager for Scottish Swimming, who both know me well. I told them I was giving up … but I asked if I could carry on training with the Scottish Disability Swim Squad with the aim of swimming just once more in competition: the British Short Course Championships in Sheffield in November. I just wanted to complete a race without incident and wash away the memory of that London one, to make sure I could finish in a better frame of mind. I knew though that I could walk away happily after that!

My last-ever competitive swim was in a relay. At that event, people went round with a programme, and lots of my friends signed it, wishing me well for the future. I still treasure it. Unknown to me, it was arranged that I should be the last swimmer in the pool. Everyone else got out of the water, and as I swam my last leg, a piper in the squad, the swimmer Hope Gordon, started playing "Flower of Scotland", a very emotional way to finally retire.

However, life goes on! Another royal garden party invitation came in for London 2013. My parents and my cousin Betty travelled down by train to London, and as usual with wheelchair travellers, we were met by a porter who made sure we were all right. It was teatime rush hour, and the Porter said, "Come with me," and ushered us right to the front of the taxi queue. There are compensations for being disabled! The day of the garden party was glorious, very sunny, and my bald patch got sunburnt. The grounds were absolutely beautiful, with rhododendrons and azaleas in full bloom in reds, yellows, and pinks. My Cousin Betty and I had our tea. We then lined up, and the Queen came in. One of the ushers told us that after the Queen had her tea, all the wheelchair people were to make their way to the pond area and one of the Royal party would speak to us. Betty and I ended up with a second tea. We spoke to the Duke of Kent and Princess Michael of Kent. On our way over, Clare Balding came up to speak to me. "It's Jim the Swim," she said and then gave me a cuddle.

I have met so many interesting people and been to so many interesting places. It is very difficult to believe that the wee skinned rabbit of a baby in an incubator could go on to achieve so much in his lifetime.

And he's not finished yet!

Random Thoughts

Mum and Dad have always believed that everyone should make the most of what they have, and not focus on what they don't have. There is no such thing as "can't". When I was growing up I was included in all aspects of family life, the good and the bad. Mum and Dad didn't shield me or overprotect me. When Ferm Granddad was very ill, we *all* went to visit. I treasured those visits and I felt part of the family. I think it's wrong if you're disabled and not allowed to laugh and grieve with the family. My cousins don't think of me as disabled. I'm just Jim, nobody special, and they expect me to be at any family occasion, happy or sad. I believe that if disabled youngsters are too sheltered, they may have difficulty coping in later life.

Mr Moyes gave a sermon one day about disabled people being cured, and it upset me. When I went home I told my mum that I didn't want to be cured. I'm quite happy being disabled because I know no different; I have been disabled from birth. People who become disabled in later life find it a lot more difficult to cope. I think they can have more problems with their disabilities than people like me. I was travelling to a Rugby International with a friend who asked me if I would still have been a swimmer if I didn't have my condition. I reacted badly to that because I don't feel as though I have a *condition*. I have a *disability*. I do not suffer from cerebral palsy; I just have it. A *condition* to me is an illness. I explained my feelings, and we ended up laughing about it.

I was brought up not to get too close to people, not to become a burden to them, and to be as independent as I can be. I keep myself to myself, but in my nature I am a worrier, quite nervous and anxious about anything and everything. This has, over the years, made me a bit of a loner and bullied at times because I was easily wound up. I sometimes think that all the difficulties I had growing up gave me something to fight against. Even in my swimming career things did not always come easily. Maybe God was telling me I had to persevere and overcome. I may be a wheelchair user, but I have a full life with lots of friends. My life is not confined to the house. It may not be a picnic, but I live it to the fullest. I hate it when people think I live in Mum's pocket. I have my life, and my parents have theirs. There are things we do together and things we do separately, as with any family.

Even if you are on the British team as an elite athlete, you should always remember your roots and support local galas. It's both encouraging to up-and-coming athletes and keeps your feet on the ground. It is my opinion that we are not getting people with more severe disabilities coming through to compete at elite levels in sport, employment, and education. As a child I competed at regional and national cerebral palsy competitions in classes for "swimmers using assistive devices". Unfortunately, this class is no longer held, and that is preventing more people with severe disability coming through to compete at local and British levels. Lottery money has meant that British Swimming has laid down achievement standards for age groups. More severely disabled competitors have more challenges to contend with in everyday living and cannot usually attain age-group standards at the proscribed age. I believe that this too is discouraging participation by less able people.

Not all people in wheelchairs are the same: they do not all need their lives organised for them; they do not all think the same way or enjoy the same things. If you're in a crowd, you are expected to follow what the crowd does. I did not like being treated as one of the crowd and made to do the same as everyone else. As a person with a disability, it sometimes feels as though you are made to fit the system rather than the system being flexible enough to adapt to your needs. Disabled people are not expected to have ambitions or to rock the boat. I first rebelled by getting my ear pierced and my hair permed.

I really get annoyed when people presume that because I have a disability I am unable to understand what is going on. I may have difficult speech that's difficult for some people to understand, but I am not brainless! I hate being patronised and like to face up to challenges. I want to be consulted and to give my opinion, especially on things that affect me and my life.

The discovery of disabled swimming opened up a whole new world to me. My eyes were opened to the fact that not everyone had to go through the New Trinity Work Centre to achieve. It brought me into contact with other people who had broken out of the stereotype of people with disabilities. People first; disability second. I met people who were holding down jobs in the Civil Service, in local government, in the media, in finance, and in so many other occupations. We could do anything, and I discovered that swimming would become my occupation.

Acknowledgements

So many people have helped me through my lifetime, and many are mentioned in my book. However, special thanks are due to those who have taken time to meet up with me to help clarify my memories and share laughter: Kenny Cairns, MBE; Eddie McCluskey, MBE; Paul Noble, MBE; and Doc Martin and Paul Wilson from Scottish Swimming.

Thanks too to Sir Chris Hoy for the foreword to my story.

Thanks to Rob Aubry, Paul McInneny, and my family for permission to use their photographs, and to Stuart Cunningham for his help in preparing them for publication.

Thanks to Broxburn Parish Church for allowing me to use their premises for some of my writing sessions.

Thanks to AuthorHouseUK for their help and guidance in the preparation of this book.

And last but by no means least, thanks to my scribe, Sally North, for her patience, perseverance, and ability to stay sane through good days and bad.

A Day with My Dad in the Mercury

On Monday morning at half past three, my dad wakes me up. I am very excited, and I only drink a cup of coffee. At four o'clock we say cheerio to Mum, and I kiss her goodbye. When we open the front door to go out, it's all very quiet and the street lights are on. We have to be very quiet too because we might waken the neighbours.

We go down to dad's workplace and park the car. He and his pal take the covers off their two lorries, and they fill in their log books. Then we are ready to start. We leave Uphall, and I can't see the fields; I can't see the back of the lorry; I can't even see my dad. He has to put his headlights on.

You must be wondering why we are so early and what we are doing. Well, my dad is a lorry driver, and we leave early to miss all the busy traffic in Glasgow. Also he has to be at Stewarton at six o'clock in the morning.

At Bathgate we see the Leyland factory. It is the only building on the road that is lit up. The night-shift workers are busy producing cars and tractors. We join the motorway – the M8 – to Glasgow. On the road it's nearly all lorries going to Glasgow market. I see the telly mast at Blackhill. We leave the M8 for another motorway before we arrive in Glasgow. It goes past Celtic Park. We see the early-morning train coming to Edinburgh. Now we are right in Glasgow. It is still quiet because it is only five o'clock in the morning. The famous shopping centre is peaceful because no people are going there yet.

There are a lot of traffic lights. They all seem to be at green. That pleases Dad. He always says, "Be at Green. Be at Green," when he comes to them because they are always on hills and he doesn't like stopping there with the heavy load at the back of the lorry. The Glasgow buses are running now. They are green at the bottom and yellow at the top.

After Glasgow we go through a lot of hills called the Fenwick Moors. It's still dark. What time is it? Half past five! We are going to schools in Stewarton. At these schools we are delivering orders of six bags of potatoes, two bags of carrots, one and a half bags of turnips, two stones of cabbage, two boxes of cookers, and about a dozen lettuce – that's a boxful – and mustard and cress for salads and parsley for soup. In the summer there's rhubarb, which I don't like.

Then we carry on to Kilmaurs and Crooked Home. They have meals-on-wheels centres. They need two tons (or forty bags) of potatoes to last them a week! They also get all the other things I've mentioned already. It's a big order, and my dad and another man carry the load in between them. If you think Crooked Home is a nice name, you will get a surprise when you go there because it is only a town full of houses like Edinburgh. At Loanhead Primary in Kilmarnock we stop for breakfast. We have a roll with cheese in it and a cup of tea. Miss W., the cook, has it all ready for us at half-past seven in her cosy kitchen.

We now have to visit twelve more schools in Kilmarnock. The big academy gets a lot of stuff. There are apples and oranges for people who are on diets. At the last school Dad gets his dinner. Sometimes he has mince eight times a week between home and school dinners! There are always potatoes. Do you fancy mince with chips? Rice pudding is his favourite and he gets it quite often. My favourite is bread and butter pudding, but I've never had it when I've been away.

It's time to come home now, and my eyes are shutting. It's only two o'clock, but I've been up since half-past three. (I've still got the BBs to go to with Mum when I get back.) I have a wee sleep while poor Dad has to drive. It's full daylight, so it is not so easy to get to sleep, but I usually manage it.

I just waken up again on the motorway when I get near home. When we reach Broxburn, Dad parks the lorry and has a wee chat to his boss before we go home.

By James Anderson, aged eleven.

THE AULD YEAR'S NICHT

One Auld Year's nicht we were sitting round the muckle fire. The clock on the mantelpiece showed eleven. Mum and Gran were sitting knitting jerseys, Dad was sleeping, and Stuart, my brother, was lying on the floor reading. Granpaw and I were just sitting.

Granpaw Jim is bald nowadays, but he used to have fair hair like me. He has a big face and a wee nose to snore well. He has old skin with lots of lines, and his eyes are bluey-grey like mine. His teeth are false, and he wears specs for reading. He's a bit of a comic and says, "I'd better get awa' tae ma bed," when he wants you to go hame. (Gran's face goes scarlet red then.)

Well, Granpaw and I were just sitting, and I said to him, "Tell me a story about your teenage years." This is what he told me:

Two months before I left the school, ma mither took me aside and said, "Me and your faither have been thinking – what about you going to Cupar Market and getting a fee? Yer faither's got the afternoon off to gang wi' ye. I've kept back some clean claes for you to put on."

So I went to Cupar Market wi' ma faither, and we roamed the streets for a while, waiting for a farmer to come up to us. The toon was filled wi' young men waiting for the words, "You want a fee?" and ready to answer, "Aye, I am."

When it was my turn the farmer said, "Let me see your character, laddie." The laddies usually had a report from the school. The farmer looked at it. "That's a guid character. I'll gie ye your milk and meal, coals and tatties, and thirty shillings a week."

"Well, laddie, are ye takin' it or no?" said ma faither.

"Oh aye, when dae ye want me to start?"

"Start as soon as ye leave school. Come awa' now. I'll buy your faither a pint."

Well I came home shouting, "Mither, I've got a fee for six months, at Broomhall Farm only five miles away. My pay will be a two-pint pitcher of milk a day, a furlett of meal, free coal and tatties, and thirty bob a week."

Ma mither said to me, "Ye ken Bob down the road? Here's some money. Awa' and buy a kist to yourself for a' yer claes. Ye can pay me back wi' your first pay."

I went out singing to masel':

> When I was only twal year auld
> I left the village school.
> Ma Faither sent me to the ploo'
> To win my milk and meal.

Well, the time was coming round when I'd to go to the bothy. My mither packed ma kist wi' claes – Sunday suit and cords for working. Schooldays were over.

For the first two days, I enjoyed the work. Nae faither walloping ma lug or sending me tae ma bed. Nae mither to say, "Wipe your feet on the mat."

Then there came a rainy morning when I got soaked at the plooing and I felt like rinning awa' hame tae ma mither. Nae clean claes, nae wee cups o' tea. I felt like rinning awa.' A' that month I felt the same, but I knew if I went hame I'd get a kick up the pants! So I stuck it oot. Then I saw a bonnie wee maid in the kitchen and that helped.

> Syne at half-five we follow our nose
> Ower tae the kitchie tae chaw our brose
> Fairm servants seldom need a dose
> O' caster ile in the morning

Now, about brose; you put meal and a teaspoon o' salt in a bowl and add boiling hot water. Ye stir it up wi' a wooden spurtle, and it's ready to eat. Grand stuff!

One day the minister came into the bothy where the farmworkers lived. The men were all sitting down to their dinner on the big scrubbed table with yesterday's paper for a tablecloth. There were pints on the table too, but they were quickly hidden under the table. Dinner was the same as breakfast and tea – brose!

The minister said, "Do you never get anything else but porridge!" The gaffer said, "We like our meat, even if it's only brose." Then they all sang "For the Beauty of the Earth" while their brose got cold!

I'll tell you mair aboot the bothy though. When I first started, ma bothy mate said, "I'll tak' the pan-a-week, seeing it's your first week at the bothy. You can do it next week."

Doing the pan-a-week meant cleaning the ashes out once a week and pushing back the fender. Pan-a-weekers rose at fower o'clock to pit on the brose. They went for coal and water. Then they made the beds from which the other men had risen in their semmets and shirt tails to draw on their work claes. There were tatties to peel into the brose pot to leave ready for Jock's wife to put on the fire.

Sometimes there was an egg for tea. The fermer kept hens, and the men often took an egg if the hens laid outside. Then they had a boil up in the tea water. The fermer never caught them, or maybe he turned a blind eye!

Inside the bothy the fireplace was high up from the floor – halfway up the wall with a space beneath for the ashes to fall. Bowls were washed out and the dirty water thrown on the ashes. The pot was a roond iron, one with a big handle over the top, and the kettle was the same, with a spout. Above the fireplace was a gas lamp fixed to the wall. It was made of brass, but the bothy men never cleaned it. There was a glass shade over the flame. On the opposite side of the mantel were pictures of our mithers. We had a food kist in the corner where we kept milk, cheese, meal, bread, jam, butter, and our brose bowls.

On a Sunday I put on ma best suit and went off hame on my pedal bike. I got a motor bike later. My first words when I got in were "Mither, here's my dirty washing!" The Sabbath was a grand day for a rest, for the rest of the week was busy on the farm.

At the sowing time we planted barley, wheat, and oats. Once there wasn't enough corn to sow the field, and so one of the young lads sowed it in bits – and when the corn came up there were bare patches all over the field! The farmer wasn't pleased, I can tell you.

At tattie time all the men went out with sacks on their backs and hand-planted the tatties with one foot pace between each. But in winter it was a thought to go out in the pouring rain to mend farm gates and other odd jobs, I can tell you.

One of the great times of year was the plooing match. Three months before it the men would be up polishing the harness. They were up all night before the match, ready to go out at five o'clock to the cuddy to feed it and groom it. Its tail was plaited and its coat polished till it shone. Then on went the bit and bells, and man and horse went out knowing there was the chance of winning a prize and better still a chance to meet old cronies.

The prize was a rosette and a certificate. I once won second prize wi' ma horse called Little – a great big brown beast. And there was always the chaffing. "That horse can't touch mine. He'll never get first prize. He can't keep a straight dreel like mine."

They started plooing two dreels and put the earth up to one side. Then the ploo had to work down one side and up the other to make a straight line to follow for the rest of the field. The judges looked for the straightest, neatest furrow and the best looking horse.

Ye want to ken mair aboot that wee kitchen lassie, do you? Well, I met up wi' her in the coo-shed. She was at the milking and I was at the dung, and I said "What aboot us going oot?"

"I hae to be in by eleven o'clock!"

"Easy."

We went to the silent movies at Leven and paid a penny to go and see Charlie Chaplin and have a cuddle in the back-row chummy seats!

But that's twelve o'clock striking. Happy New Year.

Granpaw had his dram, and we all went to our beds.

Granpaw Jim makes me laugh sometimes. He says, "Right, Jim, are ye wanting a skelp on the nose or the lug?" Then he spits on his hands and puts his fists up. He's a grand storyteller too.

By James Anderson, aged fourteen.

About the Author

James Allan Anderson, a proud Fifer, has been disabled from birth by cerebral palsy. His parents were told not to expect too much from him, as he might have learning as well as physical difficulties. They certainly couldn't have expected their son to go on to be an international swimmer at six Paralympics and countless British, European, and World Championships. Over the years Jim has won over 400 medals, including six Paralympic golds, nine Paralympic silvers, and two Paralympic bronzes. He has held numerous world records, losing his last one still standing, the 100-metre backstroke set in 2008, in 2014. He has also been inducted into the Scottish Swimming Hall of Fame. His parents could not have expected their son to be a globetrotter, visiting every continent except Antarctica! Nor could they have expected him to be decorated by the Queen not once but twice. In fact, Jim has been successful in several fields of activity, from disco-dancing to story-writing.

When he retired from competitive swimming after London 2012, Jim decided he would like to write down his life story. He continues coaching other swimmers, plays boccia, and takes his part in some athletics events.